Malcolm Hillier's
GARLANDS

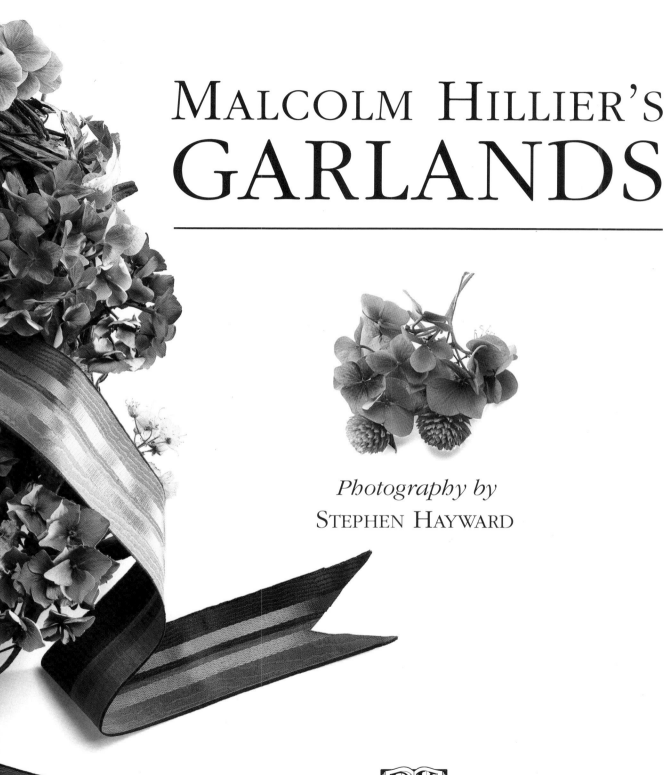

MALCOLM HILLIER'S
GARLANDS

Photography by
STEPHEN HAYWARD

DORLING KINDERSLEY
LONDON • NEW YORK • STUTTGART

A DORLING KINDERSLEY BOOK

Project Editor Gillian Roberts
Art Editor Deborah Myatt
Managing Editor Mary-Clare Jerram
Managing Art Editor Spencer Holbrook
Production Adrian Gathercole

First published in Great Britain in 1994
by Dorling Kindersley Limited
9 Henrietta Street, London WC2E 8PS

A CIP catalogue record for this book is
available from the British Library

ISBN 0-7513-0107-8

Computer page make-up by
Mark Bracey and Deborah Myatt,
Dorling Kindersley, Great Britain

Text film output by
The Right Type, Great Britain

Reproduced by
Colourscan, Singapore

Printed and bound by
Graphicom, Italy

CONTENTS

DESIGNS FOR EVERY OCCASION

FOREWORD

My introduction to the magic of garlands was when, as children, we would make daisy-chains. On those long days of summer, the lawn always seemed to be well supplied with daisies, despite my father's arduous hand-weeding sessions, and I have always had an affection for these beautiful but little considered flowers.

For this book, I've drawn together a great range of ingredients – sometimes ordinary, sometimes really exotic, but always as lovely as all plants are – to create colourful and exciting arrangements to garland and swag, to hang and drape, to swirl and entwine. There are fresh and dried flower pictures for the wall, and all manner of garlands to dress staircases, windows, fireplaces, and columns for grand celebrations and special festivities. There are simple spice and herb wreaths and other everyday decorations to hang in the kitchen, sitting room, or bedroom that will give endless pleasure not only to you, their maker, but to everyone who sees them.

You need not be an expert to enjoy a few hours' garlanding, for there's a full description of how to make everything in the book. Better still, substitute ingredients of your own choosing for those of mine, and make something that is yours in a very special way.

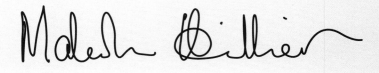

PRACTICAL ESSENTIALS

Tools and Materials
Plant Ingredients
Step-by-step Techniques

TOOLS AND MATERIALS

BEFORE YOU START making your own wreaths, garlands, and other hanging decorations, it's handy to know what tools and materials you need to have by you. Of the essential few, a really good-quality pair of florist's scissors is the most important – preferably scissors that can cut wires as well as woody plant stems.

A knife with a short, sharp-edged blade that is not too flexible; a variety of fine, medium, and stout stub wires in 30cm (12in) lengths; and a reel or two of mossing wire, are other essentials. A glue gun is a rather useful item also, making quick work of many joins that could once have been done only by wiring.

◄ WET FOAM WREATH BASE
Excellent for use with fresh flowers, these are sold in a variety of shapes and several different sizes.

DRY FOAM BALLS ▼
Use these just as they are to make hanging dried flower spheres.

THICK TWINE ▼
With its rough, slightly hairy texture, twine is ideal for non-slip ties; use also as a base for lightweight garlands.

WET FOAM BRICK ▲
These can be cut to fit into any lined container that you choose for an arrangement of fresh flowers and foliage.

STOUT CORD ▼
All but the chunkiest of flexible garlands can be wired onto stout cord.

TWISTED STEM CIRCLE ▼
Bases that are formed from natural plant materials suit both fresh and dried flowers: for speed and ease, you can buy them ready made.

RUSH HALF-BASKET WITH TWIG HANDLE ▼
Hang lush, flamboyant decorations (dried or fresh) up on a wall in a basket that has one flat side.

RAFFIA STRANDS ▼
You'll find numerous uses for raffia, from single-strand ties to plaited wreath bases.

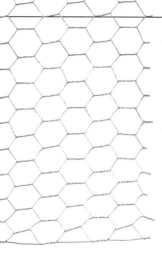

◄ CHICKEN WIRE
Moss-filled chicken wire is the base of many arrangements: use 2.5cm (1in) gauge mesh.

GUTTA PERCHA TAPE ▲
This binding tape is useful for covering wired flower stems.

A VARIETY OF RIBBONS ►
To adorn any arrangement: wire-edged ribbon holds its shape; paper ribbon is good for twirling; braid makes an ideal binding; coiled paper ribbon fans into large bows.

7cm (2¾in) wire-edged ribbon

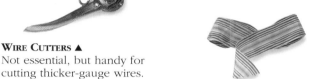

WIRE CUTTERS ▲
Not essential, but handy for cutting thicker-gauge wires.

2.5cm (1in) wire-edged ribbon

BUN MOSS ▲
The cushiony mounds dry particularly well, and retain their colour and soft texture.

SPHAGNUM MOSS ▲
Use this kind of moss as the filling for chicken-wire bases.

FLORIST'S SCISSORS ▲
A good pair will be more than worth the investment.

5cm (2in) wire-edged ribbon

CARPET MOSS ▲
Its neutral colour makes this a fine background material.

SPANISH MOSS ▲
This versatile moss comes dyed (*left*) or natural (*right*).

SECATEURS ▲
This cutting tool deals well with thick or tough stems.

SHARP KNIFE ▲
Where fresh flower stems need scraping, use a knife.

1cm (⅜in) paper ribbon

GLUE GUN AND GLUE STICKS ▼
Look for a low melt gun: it's the safest and easiest to use.

REEL WIRE ▼
Use reel (or mossing) wire for all but the finest work.

stout stub wires

medium-gauge stub wires

4cm (1½in) woven braid

ROSE WIRE ▲
Ideal for fine wiring work.

STUB WIRES ►
For wiring single heads and bunches: in several gauges.

fine stub wires

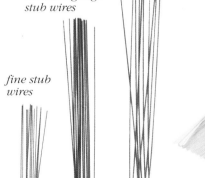

fanned, coiled paper ribbon

glue sticks

FRESH FLOWERS

ROSES, FREESIAS, DAFFODILS, carnations, and the ubiquitous chrysanthemum: look for them at your nearest florist's shop even in the depths of a hard winter and you're almost certain to find them in abundant supply. These as well as numerous other varieties are nowadays so readily available that making up fresh flower garlands for special celebrations has become an activity that's possible at any time of year.

Yet I'd still rather use flowers that have been grown in their own natural season. From the austere simplicity of winter, the freshness of springtime, the exuberance of high summer, to the glowing embers of autumn: each one of the seasons has a definite mood, which is reflected in the flowers that are about at that time. Acquaint yourself with all the different kinds to discover which you like using best.

Guernsey lily
The flowers of this nerine variety bloom in autumn, and have graceful wavy-edged petals

Dendrobium orchid
Exotic and intensely coloured, orchids are surprisingly robust

Tuberose
This summer-flowering Mexican plant has an extremely pervasive perfume

Freesia
These look delicate, but are an excellent choice for arrangements that have to last for several days or longer

Tulip
The double flowers of 'Angélique' fill the air with their sweet scent

Chrysanthemum
Spray chrysanthemums, which carry several small flowers on each stem, are more suitable for garland- and wreath-making than large single blooms

PREPARING FRESH FLOWERS

WHETHER YOU CUT flowers from your garden, or buy them from a florist's shop or market, it's always sensible to prepare them before you start to make up any arrangement. Flowers that look strong and healthy have a head start on limp, tired blooms, so pick stems that are in the very best condition. Of the more usual kinds, roses, carnations, alstroemeria, and pinks last well. Sweet peas, though wonderfully scented, fade in a day.

To condition flowers ready to use, fill a bucket or some other roomy container with cool water. With a small, sharp-bladed knife, cut the stems at an angle. Strip off lower leaves and scrape 4cm (1½in) at the ends of the stems. Place the flowers in the water, then leave them there for two hours or so. Hammer stems that are woody, such as those of lilac, after the cutting and scraping treatment.

Rose
Choose miniature or spray roses for small designs •

Golden wattle
This species of the native Australian acacias was once used for fencing, hence its name •

Carnation
The scarlet-striped petals of the carnation 'Master Stuart' make a strikingly strong statement; shown below them, sprays have less showy flowers that last just as well •

Delphinium
Purists may well insist on blue for this classic cottage-garden plant, but look out for hybrid forms in whites, pinks, lilacs, and rich purples: they're also very beautiful •

Anemone
Anemone coronaria *De Caen Series has large flat flowers of red, white, blue, or white flushed red, as here* •

FRESH FOLIAGE

IF FLOWERS ARE most often the brilliant stars in fresh arrangements, foliage forms the perfect unifying backdrop for their colourful display. Fresh foliage is there for you to choose in so broad a variety that you need never be short of the exact right thing for whatever hanging decoration you're wanting to make. Nor is it necessarily green: many species are specially grown for their attractively variegated leaves.

For cut flower decorations in vases, I always like to use the flowers' own foliage; but with garlands, it may be a different matter. Leaves of some flowers, for example carnations and roses, either are unsuitably shaped for filling in, or don't last well. So when planning your decorations, select foliage that is in harmony with them, whether it's strands of smilax for a garland or tufts of spruce for a bold swag.

Eucalyptus
Rounded, as here, or long and slender, eucalyptus leaves have a pungent, aromatic scent

Viburnum
Evergreen plants that flower in winter, like Viburnum tinus (also called laurustinus), are doubly useful

Cornus
The aptly named Cornus alba *'Elegantissima' is a species of dogwood, with deciduous, finely cream-edged leaves carried on graceful stems*

Blue spruce
Agreeably chunky, the silver-blue branches of this conifer will last for two weeks or so out of water: such foliage is perfect for care-free, long-holiday decorations

Hebe
Splashes of creamy-white brighten the evergreen leaves of this compact, bushy shrub

PREPARING FRESH FOLIAGE

ALL FRESH FOLIAGE needs some preparation if it's to last. Run some tepid water into a bucket or other roomy container: a small amount will do. Cut the stems across at an angle, using a sharp knife, and scrape 4cm (1½in) at the bottom of each one. For woody stems only, hammer their ends. Leave the foliage in the water for at least two hours; if your schedule allows, overnight is even better. Foliage that starts to look tired can be revived by putting already prepared stems into very hot water. After five minutes, top up the hot with cold water and leave the foliage to condition as described above.

Smilax
Climbers almost twine themselves through garlands

Bells of Ireland
The leaves of this plant are of less interest than the large green calyx that surrounds each flower spike

Fishtail palm
Unusual leaves add a touch of drama to fresh arrangements of uncomplicated plant materials

Rosemary
Hang herby wreaths where they can waft their scent: aromatic foliage readily yields up its perfume when brushed against or crushed

Cypress
Sprays of compact and spreading foliage make a good background for flat wall hangings

Tree ivy
This vigorous ivy hybrid has glossy evergreen leaves; its white autumn flowers give way to black fruits

Tree asparagus
Frothy tufts suit any delicate design

DRIED PLANT MATERIAL

IT MAKES EXCELLENT SENSE to use dried flowers and foliage, seedheads and pods in many of your garlands, swags, and hanging creations. Arrangements that have taken hours of work to put together will never flag or expire, and you can make them whenever you like from materials that are always available. But don't keep them for more than nine months or so: after this time they begin to look a trifle sad.

Flower markets, garden centres, and florists, and even some shops specializing in interior design and homewares, are all worth a look into for the tantalizing selection of dried and preserved plant material that's nowadays for sale. Cultivating plants yourself, either in the garden or in containers, then drying them, is a satisfying way of obtaining those particular ingredients that you want to use most often.

Miniature globe thistle
Spiky leaves set off these steel-blue heads

Artemisia
This tall plant is grown for its willowy silver-grey foliage

Cluster-flowered everlasting
Like all everlastings, this variety is superb for drying

Larkspur
Cultivated plants can be blue, white, or pink, but their wild cousins are usually violet

Field poppy
With their crisp, strong form, poppy seedheads work best in designs of bold materials

Sunflower
Dried blooms keep all the brilliance of fresh flowers: the crumpled petals swiftly perk up in a cloud of steam

STEAMING FLOWERS

Revive dried flowers that are squashed by holding them in the steam of a boiling kettle. Their petals will start to flop in moments. Holding the flower away from the steam and upside down, blow up quite gently into the petals: the shape is soon set.

after: revived

before: squashed

Strelitzia •
Palm-like bird-of-paradise leaves dry into wonderfully twisted and sinuous shapes

Lavender
If you're growing this scented favourite to dry yourself, pick stems as the flowers begin to open for the best results •

Rose
Rosa 'Golden Time', a modern hybrid tea rose, bears its compact, open flowers on abundantly leafy stems •

Yarrow
Any arrangement of dried plant materials is certain to make a major statement if it includes these large flat heads of golden flowers •

Statice
These fanned clusters of very small flowers come in numerous shades of blue, red, white, yellow, and purple •

Copper beech
Preserving in glycerine
will keep foliage pliant;
this had a bit of purple
dye added to enhance
its natural colouring
• of bronze-red

Dutch rush
Also known as mare's
tails, these decorative
dried stems are from
a plant best kept out
of the garden: it's a
• rampant weed

Celosia cockscomb
The rich reds, yellows,
oranges, and purples
of these velvety crests
glint with a lustrous
• silver sheen

Prince's feather
Tall and bushy, the flower
spires of this amaranthus
species may be coloured
burgundy-red, as here,
• or pink or green

Bottlebrush
The scarlet clusters
that surround these
stems are the showy
slender stamens of
tiny flowers •

PRESERVING FLOWERS AND FOLIAGE

PRESERVING FLOWERS and foliage yourself is not at all difficult. Many well-known flower species can simply be hung up, heads down, to dry in a cool and dark place. Strawflowers, statice, the hybrid tea roses, and larkspur can be dried in this way, and last very well. Be certain there's no hint of damp, or the flowers will go mouldy before they've entirely dried out. Encase flowers like peonies, lilies, and lovely old-fashioned roses in crystals of silica gel for the best results.

As for foliage: that of beech, oak, and ivy responds particularly well to being preserved in glycerine. Add a dash of dye in an appropriate shade, if you want, to provide the foliage with lasting colour of a good density. If you become really interested in the drying of plant materials, consult one of the many books available. My *Complete Book of Dried Flowers* gives the techniques in detail, and design guidelines too.

Miniature honesty
The branching stems of Lunaria minima *are covered in a mass of beautiful lime-green rustling seedheads*

Rose
The subtle creamy-pink shades of Rosa *'Europa' become even softer when the blooms dry*

Love-in-a-mist
Dried just as the flower petals fall, these seedheads will be at their plum-green best

Strawflower
Aglow with vibrant colour, strawflowers make a magnificent garden display and dry superbly well

Sunray
Dainty Helipterum roseum *dries just as easily as the related strawflower*

Tree ivy
Given the glycerine and dye treatment, this evergreen plant has all the vigour of fresh foliage

FRUITS AND VEGETABLES

A LEISURELY STROLL through a farmer's or open market will furnish you with a whole host of wonderful new ideas for wreath and garland ingredients. So often, we shop for vegetables and fruits thinking of them only as food that we tend to forget just how beautiful are their natural forms and colours. Even a leaf of the humble cabbage creates a marvellous effect.

Consider vicious red chillies; dark purple exotic mangosteens; cloves of garlic flushed pink through their tight papery skins; sticks of woodsy cinnamon bark; the sculpture of tropical pods. Possibilities soon appear if you let your imagination wander a little.

String of garlic
The compact heads are a superb shape, but do carry a perfume that's not to everyone's taste

Physalis
This member of the tomato family is also called Cape gooseberry: pull back the petal-like calyx to reveal the juicy orange fruits

Bird's eye chillies
You can thread these together for Christmas tree garlands, or wire them into wreaths for a kitchen or pantry

Cinnamon bark
Braid-tied bundles are a fragrant addition to herb and spice wreaths

Pink pepperberries
Not genuine peppercorns, but still an edible seasoning, these decorative trusses are the fruit of the shrub, Schinus molle

Baby globe artichoke
These specially cultivated, miniature editions of the full-sized vegetables are best used fresh

Savoy cabbage
Add a dramatic touch to an otherwise plain design with a leaf of deep-etched veins and crinkles

Walnuts in shell
Hard-shelled nuts can
be burnished with gold
or silver spray paint

Tropical seedpods
Groups of these fascinating
objects make decorations
of spectacular simplicity

Pattypan squash
Use bite-sized vegetables
for small-scale designs

Whiteheart cherry
Fruits in pairs are easy
to hook into garlands

Tamarillo
Ruby-red fruits are a
must for festive swags

Fir and pine cones
These can look rustic or grand,
depending on how you use them

Dried mushroom cone
The edges are thin and
brittle: handle with care

Hop vines
Hang garlands made with these
trails away from the hurly-burly
of a crowd, or they will become
crushed and disintegrate

Pomegranate
Heavy fruits like these
should be hollowed out
before being wired into
an arrangement

Crab apples
Unblemished fruits on
the stem last a couple
of weeks out of water

Mangosteen
The thick, fibrous skin
of this Malaysian fruit
encloses juicy segments
of sweet-acid flesh

Lime
Lift ingredients of subdued
tints by mixing them with
one vibrant colour

Red chillies
No matter that these wrinkle
as they dry: their shiny
redness blazes on

Clementines
The attractiveness of citrus
fruits is doubled when the
leaves are still attached

WIRING PLANT MATERIAL

OFTEN, YOU CAN MAKE UP wreaths, swags, and hanging arrangements using fresh and dried flowers and leaves on their own stems. With some designs, however, you will want to be able to get a single flower or bunch to lie or point just so, in one particular direction, and this is where wiring plant material comes in. Although most wiring techniques are not at all hard to do, some can be a little bit tricky.

If you have a substantial amount of wiring to do, such as when making up several lengths of garlanding, leave yourself lots of time – it isn't a quick job. Four of the sequences here illustrate easy techniques that you can use to attach either individual pieces or bunches of plant material into a wreath or garland base. Where a visibly neat, tidy finish is important, complete your work using gutta percha tape.

WIRING A SHORT, FRAGILE, OR WOODY STEM

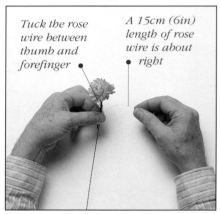

Tuck the rose wire between thumb and forefinger

A 15cm (6in) length of rose wire is about right

1 Hold the stem and a stub wire together. Put a piece of rose wire parallel to them.

Rotate the stem and stub wire between your thumb and forefinger

Keep a taut hold of the rose wire

2 Twist the rose wire, from its midpoint, up the stem. Wind it over itself at the top.

Finish a little way beyond the end of the stem

3 Continue to twist the wire down over itself, the stub wire, and length of the stem.

WIRING A BUNCH OF DRIED OR FRESH PLANT MATERIAL

Choose a 35cm (14in) stub wire that's strong enough to support the bunch

1 Place a stub wire against the stems and extending above the head of the bunch.

Spiralling the wire over itself holds it securely

2 Bend the long end of the stub wire across the front of the bunch, then around it.

Wired bunches are easily fixed into any base

Stub-wire tail

3 Twist the wire over itself down to the ends of the stems, leaving a longish tail.

WIRING A SOFT STEM

Leave a tail if you want to wire the flower into a bunch

Light flowers need a medium-gauge wire, heavy ones a stout wire

1 Push a length of stub wire up through the middle of the stem and into the flower.

WIRING EITHER A HOLLOW OR A SOFT STEM

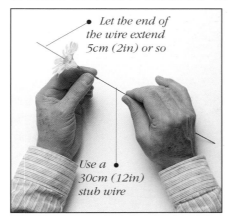

Let the end of the wire extend 5cm (2in) or so

Use a 30cm (12in) stub wire

1 Push a length of stub wire up through the stem, then on beyond the flower head.

The loop is hidden and held firmly in the flower centre

2 Bend a loop in the end of the stub wire. Pull it back into the centre of the flower.

USING GUTTA PERCHA TAPE

FOR SOME VERY SPECIAL arrangements, you may want to get a finish that withstands close scrutiny. Bridal headdresses, for example, are seen from all sides and angles, even from underneath. With designs of this sort, it's best to hide the rather unsightly stems of wired flowers and leaves. You can do this by covering them with gutta percha tape. This is available in pale or dark green or brown for colour-matching to the flower stem and looks quite natural.

Bridal headdress, upperside

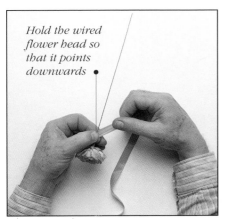

Hold the wired flower head so that it points downwards

1 Lay a piece of gutta percha tape, at an angle, close to the base of the wired flower.

Keep a tension on the tape with your free hand as you twirl the stem

2 Twirl the flower stem with one hand so that the tape spirals tightly down the stem.

Bridal headdress, underside

Gutta percha tape covers the flower stems and the wire that binds them to the stub-wire base of this bridal headdress

FLEXIBLE BASE TECHNIQUES

IF THE GARLAND you are wanting to make is to frame a window or doorway; hang in swags against a wall or table front; or spiral around a column or pole, it is best to put it together on a flexible base such as wire, stout twine, light cord, or soft rope. All are excellent for dainty, lightweight garlands of fresh flowers.

The basic technique for making garlands of this kind is simple. Before you start on one of these projects, though, bear in mind that it takes some while to make a long garland. Set aside several hours if you want to do it in one go. Garlands of heavy plant material are best made on a rigid base *(see page 26)*.

MAKING A GARLAND ON A STOUT TWINE BASE

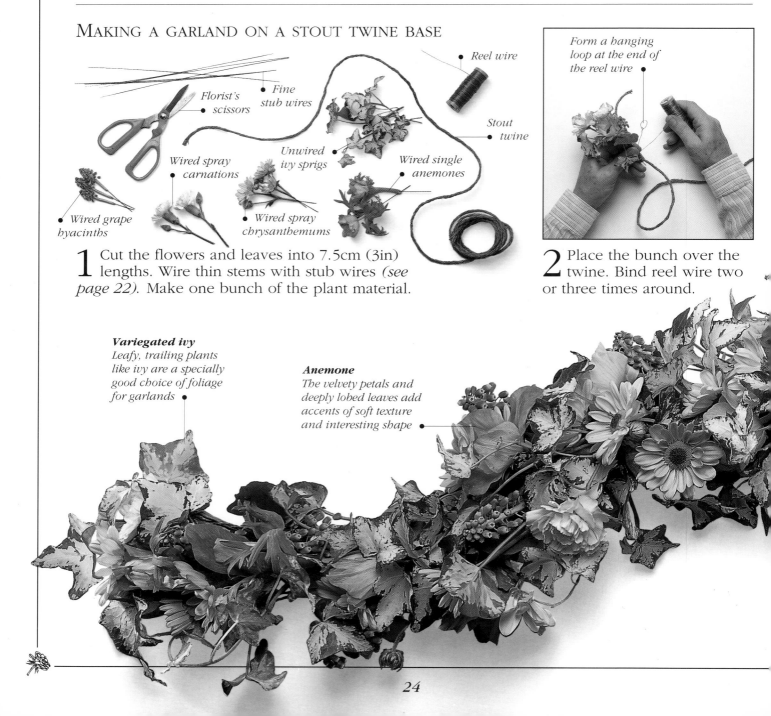

Reel wire

Florist's scissors

Fine stub wires

Stout twine

Wired spray carnations

Unwired ivy sprigs

Wired single anemones

Wired grape hyacinths

Wired spray chrysanthemums

Form a hanging loop at the end of the reel wire

1 Cut the flowers and leaves into 7.5cm (3in) lengths. Wire thin stems with stub wires *(see page 22)*. Make one bunch of the plant material.

2 Place the bunch over the twine. Bind reel wire two or three times around.

Variegated ivy
Leafy, trailing plants like ivy are a specially good choice of foliage for garlands

Anemone
The velvety petals and deeply lobed leaves add accents of soft texture and interesting shape

A firm turn of the wire around the back of the bunch holds it in place

• *Add bunch after bunch to finish the garland*

3 Pass the wire spool back up between the bunch and the twine, then pull it down on the other side. This stops the wire unravelling.

4 Make another bunch of the plant material. Put it over the first bunch so that its head overlaps the stems of the previous bunch.

Grape hyacinth
These delicate spring flowers have the scent of creamy sweet butter

Spray carnation
Full flowers with many layers of petals help to fill in any gaps

Spray chrysanthemum
Available all year round in many colours, these last well out of water

The final bunch
Reverse the direction of the final bunch so that the garland will have two flowery ends

RIGID BASE TECHNIQUES

ALL WREATHS are best made up on some kind of a rigid base, which will easily support the flowers, foliage, fruits, seedheads, and other plant material that you want to place into it. The most useful and versatile base is a tube made of chicken wire rolled around a solid stuffing of dry sphagnum moss. Use this for making heavy garlands and swags also. Just leave the two tube ends unjoined, and then bend the tube to the shape that you require.

A copper-wire frame clad with moss can be used for a lightweight wreath. If you want a base that is quick to do and looks lovely in its own right, a ring of plaited raffia may be your choice. All these bases are suitable for use with dried ingredients. Wreaths of fresh flowers need a wet foam base *(see page 74)*, especially if they contain short-lived flowers. Designs that call for solid shapes are easy to make on a mattress base *(see pages 30–31)*.

MAKING A CIRCULAR CHICKEN WIRE AND MOSS BASE

Snip the chicken wire to the size you need with wire cutters

Reel wire

Florist's scissors

Dry sphagnum moss

Wire cutters

1 Slightly flatten the chicken wire and lay it on a firm surface. Put the moss along one long side, distributing it evenly.

Secure the tube by bending the spiky snipped ends into the moss

Press the roll into shape as you go

2 Starting from one end, roll the chicken wire with the moss to get a thin, firm tube.

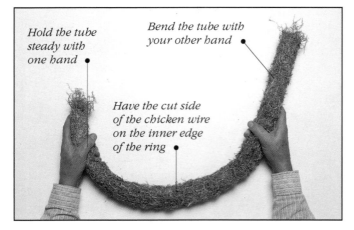

Hold the tube steady with one hand

Bend the tube with your other hand

Have the cut side of the chicken wire on the inner edge of the ring

3 Grasp the tube with both hands and, again working from one end, bend it around so that the two ends butt together to form a ring.

Use the free end of wire to lace the two tube ends together

4 Join up the ring by running reel wire back and forth from one end of the tube to the other. Cut the wire and neatly tie off its ends.

COVERING A SHOP-BOUGHT WIRE FRAME WITH MOSS

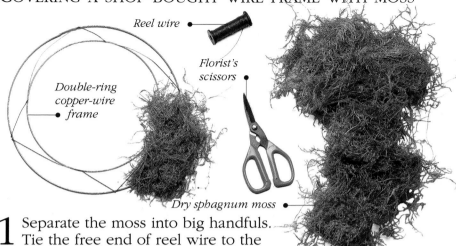

Reel wire

Florist's scissors

Double-ring copper-wire frame

Dry sphagnum moss

To finish, tie off the reel wire to the first knot, and tuck the two ends into the moss

1 Separate the moss into big handfuls. Tie the free end of reel wire to the outer ring of the frame in a firm knot.

2 Using reel wire, bind the handfuls of moss to the frame to cover it completely.

MAKING A PLAITED RAFFIA RING

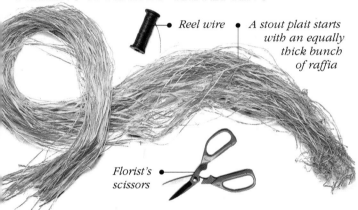

Reel wire

A stout plait starts with an equally thick bunch of raffia

Florist's scissors

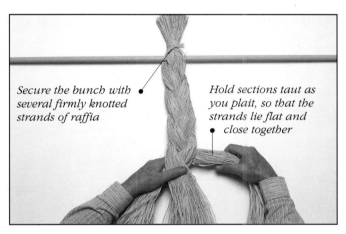

Secure the bunch with several firmly knotted strands of raffia

Hold sections taut as you plait, so that the strands lie flat and close together

1 Prepare a thick bunch of raffia by combing through the length with your fingers. This separates the strands and untangles any knots.

2 Bind one end of the bunch and tie it to a firm support. Divide into three. Plait left and right alternately over the centre section.

Tidy up the plait by cutting off any short strands of raffia that stick out

Leave straggly ends on the loop, or cut them off if you prefer a neater finish

3 Holding on to the free end, untie the plait from its support. Cross over the two ends, forming a ring. Secure the join with reel wire.

4 Plait a thin raffia bunch for a hanging loop. Tie it over the join, and cross its two ends into a bow. Bind with a single strand of raffia.

COVERING A CHICKEN WIRE AND MOSS BASE

Handmade chicken wire and dry moss wreath base

15cm (6in) medium-gauge stub wires

Spanish moss, dyed green

35cm (14in) stout stub wire

Florist's scissors

Drape the moss over the ring to cover both edges

Stub-wire hairpins

1 Make the base *(see page 26)*. Separate the Spanish moss into thick strands. Bend the medium stub wires in half to form hairpins.

2 Attach the moss: push the hairpins through the base, then bend their ends back in.

Keep the ends 2.5cm (1in) apart as you push them through

Wire loop for hanging

Give the wire end a final firm tug away from the base before bending it back

Bend up the wire loop to hang the wreath

3 Twist a loop in the centre of the stout stub wire. Push both ends from the back of the base, at top mid-centre, through to the front.

4 Holding onto the twisted wire centre, bend one of the ends, then push it back into the base. Secure the second end in the same way.

Wreath base, covered with Spanish moss

Wired bunches of dried flowers and preserved leaves

Florist's scissors

Wired single fir cones

Unwired single dried peony heads, refreshed in steam

Push the wire through and back in to the base

5 Refresh dried flowers (optional, *see page 17*). Wire single cones, and bunches of the dried flowers and foliage *(see page 22)*.

6 Arrange the background (here, cones) in a pattern that is balanced yet informal.

All the bunches should face the same way

Flowers with strong stalks are simply pushed in: no need to wire them

7 Push in the next layer (here, preserved ivy, with dried strawflowers and roses in wired bunches). Keep the colours evenly distributed.

8 Add the last layer (here, single large heads of dried peonies). Using two shades of the same colour gives the design an extra interest.

Peony
Dried flowers often have squashed petals, but will blossom again if bathed in a cloud of steam

Fir cone
Wire cones without stalks by twisting a stub wire around the scales at the base

Ivy
Preserved in a solution of glycerine and green dye, these have all the suppleness and glossy colour of fresh leaves

Rose
Store deep-coloured dried flowers in a nest of acid-free tissue paper

Strawflower
Growing these is little bother, and they dry beautifully

MAKING A CHICKEN WIRE AND MOSS MATTRESS BASE

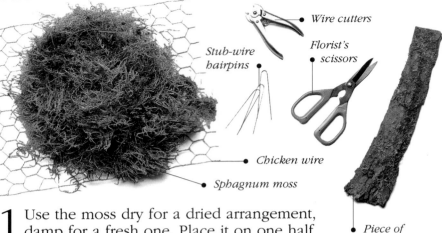

Wire cutters

Stub-wire hairpins

Florist's scissors

Chicken wire

Sphagnum moss

Piece of tree bark

First corner, bent into a curve

Press the spiky wire edges into the moss

1 Use the moss dry for a dried arrangement, damp for a fresh one. Place it on one half of the chicken wire, in about the right shape.

2 Fold over the other half of chicken wire. Bend in the four corners to create a circle.

Pin across the wire mesh, not through the holes

Secure the bark (or other object) in at least two places

3 For a large mattress, push in a number of stub-wire hairpins to hold the moss firmly in place. Space them apart at regular intervals.

4 To attach a piece of bark (or other object), thread a medium-gauge stub wire through the wire base. Tie it tightly around the object.

ATTACHING THE DECORATIVE PLANT MATERIAL

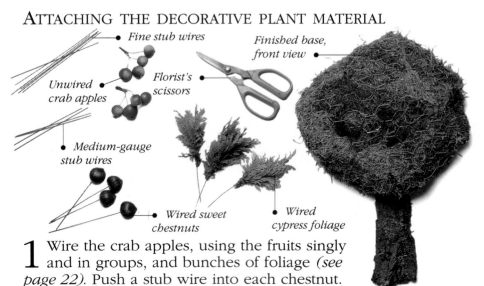

Fine stub wires

Unwired crab apples

Florist's scissors

Finished base, front view

Medium-gauge stub wires

Wired sweet chestnuts

Wired cypress foliage

Central bunches stick up

Fan out side bunches

1 Wire the crab apples, using the fruits singly and in groups, and bunches of foliage *(see page 22)*. Push a stub wire into each chestnut.

2 Push the foliage into the base. Overlap each layer so that the stems are hidden.

For an extra firm fixing, poke in the wire at an oblique angle

3 Wire in the nuts, pushing the stub wire of each nut all the way through the mattress base. Bend it back into the moss to secure it.

Mix the fruits in bunches, pairs, and singly

4 Attach the crab apples, again pushing their stub wires through and back into the base. Add more fruits and nuts for a balanced effect.

Sweet chestnut
Put a dot of strong glue on the end of the stub wire, if necessary, to keep it in place

Cypress
Choose plant ingredients that will work with you to achieve the look you're after: the soft, flattened sprays of aromatic cypress foliage fall in place almost by themselves

Crab apple
Groups and single fruits create a pleasing pattern that looks spontaneous yet well balanced

Filling the gaps
When the arrangement appears finished, prop it upright and stand back: holes and gaps that you may not have seen close to are usually revealed from a distance

Bark
A single ingredient of interest may be the starting point for a whole arrangement: my tree idea came from this mossy piece of bark

DESIGNS FOR EVERY OCCASION

Wreaths, Rings, Circlets
Garlands, Swags, Festoons
Hanging Plant Pictures

Aromatic Herb Wreath

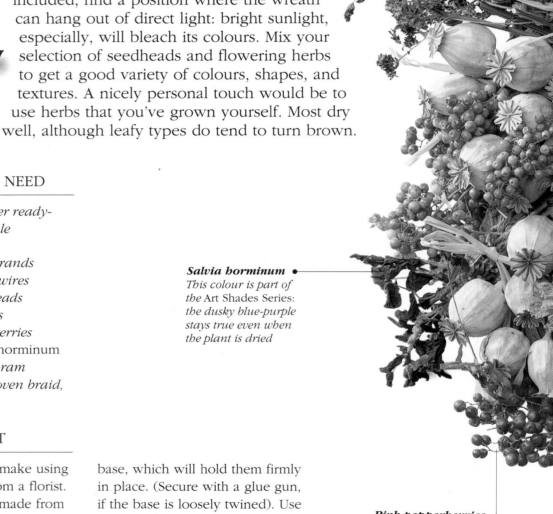

The kitchen is the perfect place to hang this colourful wreath of dried country herbs and spices. Choose a door or wall near your food preparation area, but away from steam and moisture, where you can enjoy its sweetly aromatic perfume while you are working. If you decide to use very bright flowers, like the African marigolds that I've included, find a position where the wreath can hang out of direct light: bright sunlight, especially, will bleach its colours. Mix your selection of seedheads and flowering herbs to get a good variety of colours, shapes, and textures. A nicely personal touch would be to use herbs that you've grown yourself. Most dry well, although leafy types do tend to turn brown.

What you will need

- *35cm (14in) diameter ready-made twisted stem circle*
- *Glue gun (optional)*
- *Few natural raffia strands*
- *Medium-gauge stub wires*
- *60 field poppy seedheads*
- *20 African marigolds*
- *4 stalks pink pepperberries*
- *25 stems blue* Salvia horminum
- *50 stems sweet marjoram*
- *2m (6½ft) orange woven braid, 4cm (1½in) wide*

Salvia horminum •
This colour is part of the Art Shades Series: *the dusky blue-purple stays true even when the plant is dried*

Pink pepperberries •
Slightly piquant in taste, these berries come from a small shrub native to South America

How to make it

This wreath is easy to make using a twisted stem base from a florist. I've chosen one that's made from thick vine stems twined together. Cut the stems of the poppy heads and marigolds at an angle – make each stem about 15cm (6in) long. Wire the pepperberries into small bunches *(see page 22)*. Now push the poppy and marigold stems in between the stems of the wreath base, which will hold them firmly in place. (Secure with a glue gun, if the base is loosely twined). Use strands of raffia to tie on bunches of salvia and marjoram, threading the raffia through two or three of the base stems and tying the ends into small, neat bows. Wire in the bunches of pink pepperberries by their tails. Complete the design by winding braid around the wreath.

• **Marjoram**
The variety called sweet
marjoram is especially
aromatic, and will
scent the air all
around the wreath

• **African marigold**
Traditional, cottagey
flowers like marigolds
are a good choice for
informal designs

Woven braid
Decorate your wreath
with rustic braiding
that complements its
• natural ingredients

• **Field poppy**
The neutral shade of
the seedheads helps
bring the stronger
colours to life

CORNFLOWER GARLAND

DELICATE GARLANDS AND FESTOONS look most attractive when they are twisted around the narrow pole of a marquee, looped along the front of a buffet table, or are used to frame a small window or doorway. If a garland is to hang loose, I find it best to attach the flowers into a slender base framework of chicken wire and moss *(see page 86, FRUITED HOLLY FESTOON)*, for on a flexible cord base like the one here, the heavier flowers always turn around and flop downwards.

WHAT YOU WILL NEED

FOR EVERY 1M (39IN) OF GARLAND
- *1m (39in) stout cord*
- *Medium-gauge stub wires*
- *Reel wire*
- *12 lychee fruits*
- *60 heads blue cornflowers*
- *15 sprigs feverfew*
- *12 stems* Protea *'Blushing Bride'*
- *15 sprigs gypsophila*
- *3 strands smilax*

HOW TO MAKE IT

This garland is made on a FLEXIBLE BASE *(see pages 24–25)*.
Push a short length of stub wire into the base of each lychee fruit. Make up small bunches of all the flowers, adding the fruits as well. Bind each bunch to the cord with reel wire as you go, overlapping its head with the stems of the last. Dress any gaps with extra flowers. Twine smilax through the garland (get a friend to help with this).

Cornflower
These come also in red, pink, white, and mauve, but the familiar blue flowers are still my favourites

Gypsophila •
This variety, 'Bristol Fairy', is a light-as-air cobweb of double white flowers held on the finest of stems

Lychee
The wonderfully textured
and colourful skin encloses
a deliciously scented, edible
• fruit with a glossy seed

Smilax
This scrambling foliage
plant is grown on fine
• strands of cotton

Protea 'Blushing Bride'
A miniature, somewhat
less usual form of protea,
with flowers of the most
• delicate ice-pink

Feverfew
The daisy-like flowers, also
known as bachelor's buttons,
are an old herbal remedy for
• relieving aches and pains

CELOSIA SPHERES

ADD A FOCUS OF INTEREST to a plain bedroom or study with one of these richly colourful dried flower spheres. Although they are a little time-consuming to put together, they are not at all hard to make. Choose your own combination of colours, but be sure to use a good variety of different flowers, leaves, and seedheads to give a range of shapes and textures to the finished arrangement. My raspberry-pink celosia and blackberry-coloured strawflowers with steely-blue globe thistles make a lively and exciting partnership.

WHAT YOU WILL NEED

FOR ONE HANGING SPHERE
- *10cm (4in) diameter dry foam sphere*
- *Medium-gauge stub wires*
- *Glue gun*
- *Reindeer moss*
- *15 maroon roses*
- *15 dark red roses*
- *15 pink miniature roses, including some buds*
- *15 miniature globe thistles*
- *5 stems purple statice (optional)*
- *10 stems pink celosia cockscomb*
- *10 stems maroon strawflowers*
- *2m (6½ft) wire-edged ribbon, 5cm (2in) wide*

HOW TO MAKE IT

Bend a 35cm (14in) stub wire in half. Push the two ends through the dry foam sphere. Cut a piece of ribbon 60cm (24in) long and thread it through the wire loop. Secure the ribbon by pulling the wire ends tight and bending them back into the base of the sphere.

Miniature globe thistle
The dense, compact heads are sharply spiked when dried

Glue on reindeer moss to cover the sphere, then hang it up by the ribbon at an easy working height. You can push all the roses, globe thistles, and statice easily into the sphere, as they have strong stems. The weak-stemmed strawflowers and fat-stemmed celosia must be glued into place, though. Balance the arrangement for both colour and texture, keeping an informal feel. Attach wired ribbon tails or loops to the sphere at either end.

Miniature rose
Choose tight buds on strong stems, and include some of their leaves

Ribbon bow
A small bow at the base is an integral part of the design

Decorative tails
I made the pretty zig-zag edging of these tails by cutting the ribbon with dressmaker's pinking shears

Multi-looped bow
Flamboyant bows with perky, unfloppy loops are easy to achieve if you use ribbon that's wired at the edge

Statice
Put in these delicate, flowery clusters if you want an arrangement with a less sombre look

Strawflower
Ever popular, and available in a huge colour range to match almost any room scheme

Celosia cockscomb
The soft, velvety squirls and vivid colours of the celosia plumes contrast with the spiny texture and subtle hues of the globe thistles

Sweet Pea Wreath

There is nothing quite as beautiful as the scent of sweet peas, and no other flower perfume is quite like it. The beginning of the season, just as summer gets into full swing, is the best time for them. Then, their flowers are held on strong stalks; their blooms last a little better; and their scent is as intense as it ever gets. For this charming fresh flower wreath, I've matched sweet peas in shades of lavender with lilac-coloured statice. The foliage and minuscule flowers of snow-in-summer provide bright touches of silvery green, white and yellow. Hang the completed wreath in any setting where it can be easily seen and admired. If you are entertaining, your guests will remember, with pleasure and for many summers to come, the heady scent and subtle colours of your sweet pea wreath.

Paper ribbon •
Excellent for twirling into curls and twists that hold their shape

What you will need

- *30cm (12in) diameter circular wet foam wreath base*
- *10 stems snow-in-summer foliage, including some flowers*
- *40 stems pale & darker lavender-coloured sweet peas*
- *15 stems lilac-coloured statice*
- *2m (6½ft) green & white paper ribbon, 1cm (⅜in) wide*

Sweet pea •
Lovely but short-lived, the deliciously scented sweet pea traditionally symbolizes both delicate pleasure and departure

How to make it

Sweet peas last only two or three hours out of water before starting to wilt, so it is best to arrange the flowers in a wet foam base. Soak the base in water until the foam is damp through. The base will drip when hung up if you oversoak it. Trim the foliage and flower stems into sprigs about 15cm (6in) long. Put in the foliage first, spacing it evenly around the circle. Keep a few sprigs aside to fill in any gaps later on. Place the sweet peas and statice among the foliage, either in bands spiralling across the wreath, as I've done, or at random. Fill in with the foliage sprigs that you set aside, so that the foam is entirely hidden. Complete the wreath with curlicues of narrow paper ribbon.

Statice •
Paler shades, like the lilac I've chosen, suit the tissue-thin petals of statice best, though the flowers come in bolder colour variants

Snow-in-summer
*Use stems with a good
mix of variegation:
the topmost leaves
have the broadest
• white margins*

SIMPLE SUNFLOWER SHAPES

FOR SPECIAL OCCASIONS, DECORATIONS THAT ARE wonderfully opulent, rich, and extravagant have a great appeal; but for everyday, it's nice to have something less outspoken up your sleeve – something with a simplicity of form and colour that's comfortable to live with, yet that still holds your attention. My triangle and diamond are unfussy shapes, made from bundles of raffia-tied stems decorated with dried seedheads and flowers in woodsy colours. Hanging up in your kitchen or hallway, they make an out-of-the-ordinary decoration that will last for a year or so. Give them an occasional gentle blow with a hairdryer to keep any dust at bay.

WHAT YOU WILL NEED

FOR BOTH SUNFLOWER SHAPES
- *Natural raffia strands, for tying*
- *Glue gun*

FOR THE SUNFLOWER TRIANGLE
- *18 stems Dutch rush,*
30cm (12in) long, in 3 bundles
- *5 dried sunflowers*
- *10 heads craspedia*
- *2 heads leucadendron*
- *3 heads Protea compacta*
- *6 scabious seedheads, with bells removed from 3 of them*

FOR THE SUNFLOWER DIAMOND
- *28 stems red cornus,*
50cm (20in) long, in 4 bundles
- *9 sunflowers*
- *7 heads leucadendron*
- *9 heads Protea mellifera*
- *3 heads Protea compacta*

HOW TO MAKE THEM

Using raffia strands, bind together the bundles of stems, 4cm (1½in) or so from their ends. Cut all the flower- and seedhead-stalks short. Glue everything in place, pushing the glued stalks between the base stems so that they are firmly held. Cut off entirely any stalks that are too thick to push in, and glue the flower by its base onto the stems.

Craspedia
Each globular head of these saffron-coloured flowers makes a bold contribution to the arrangement

Dutch rush
The hard, quite rigid stems of this native British plant are ideal for binding into a simple wreath base

Sunflower
When dried, the flower petals crinkle prettily, and keep their warm, glowing colour

Scabious
These seedheads look like many little bells nestling together

Scabious
The seedheads still look good without the fragile bells

Protea mellifera
*Continue the protea theme,
but don't let it get boring,
by choosing larger flowers
• of a different species*

Natural raffia tie
*Make visible joins into
a pleasing feature of the
design by using a natural
material, like this raffia,
to bind the stems together •*

Protea compacta •
*Dried protea flowers have
petals with an oddly woody
texture and pincushion-
like centres*

• Leucadendron
*The spiky form of these
cones is softened by the
pure white, fluffy seeds*

Cornus stems
*The rich mahogany-red
colour of the stems is an
all-season attraction of
• this dogwood species*

HEDGEROW WITH TREE

BRING BACK MEMORIES OF SUMMER with this stunning countryside scene, made on a mattress base and using sticks, moss, and dried flowers to create the hedgerow, gate, and tree. Do not be daunted by what may look like an ambitious project, but do set aside several hours to make it. Display the finished plaque against a wall, either sitting on a mantelshelf or hanging like a picture. The flowers you choose to decorate the tree canopy can suit your own colour scheme. I used yarrow, a super match for my yellow dining room walls *(see pages 46–47)*.

WHAT YOU WILL NEED

FOR THE HEDGEROW
- *2 pieces chicken wire, 80cm (32in) long & 15cm (6in) wide*
- *8 handfuls dry sphagnum moss*
- *Medium-gauge stub wires, bent into hairpins 10cm (4in) long*
- *Carpet moss*
- *Bun moss*
- *Silver reindeer moss*
- *6 fronds cress seedheads*
- *6 sprigs pink campion*
- *6 scabious seedheads*
- *4 blue cornflowers*

FOR THE FRAME & GATE
- *Heavy-duty staple gun*
- *8 thin wooden struts, 10cm (4in) long*
- *Two 2cm (¾in) diameter straight branches, 1m (39in) long*
- *Four 1.2cm (½in) diameter gateposts, 10cm (4in) long, sharpened to a point at one end*
- *One 1.2cm (½in) diameter crossbar, 13cm (5in) long*

FOR THE TREE
- *1 piece chicken wire, 60cm (24in) long & 15cm (6in) wide*
- *2 handfuls dry sphagnum moss*
- *One 3cm (1¼in) diameter branched trunk, 30cm (12in) long*
- *6 handfuls green Spanish moss*
- *5 large heads yarrow, divided into several small florets*

HOW TO MAKE IT

This wall hanging is made on a MATTRESS BASE *(see pages 30–31)*. Make two moss-filled mattresses for the hedgerow. Screw the eight struts to the two straight branches to form a frame, leaving a gap of 18cm (7in) for the gate. Staple a hedge at each end. Screw on the four upright gateposts, then the diagonal crossbar. Attach all the plant material with wire hairpins. Make a moss-filled mattress for the tree canopy and staple it to the trunk. Screw to a hedge through the frame. Attach Spanish moss and yarrow to the tree canopy with wire hairpins.

Cress
Let tall stalks peep up over the hedge •

Bun moss
Creates a splendid 3-D effect •

Spanish moss
The kind I've used
has been dyed a
soft green •

Yarrow florets
Dress the tree canopy
• with vivid flowers

**Pink campion
flowers**
Include spots of
• a pale colour

Scabious seedhead
Clustered seedheads
• add a new texture

Tree trunk •
This branched piece
of mahonia makes
an interesting stem

Blue cornflower
Brings vitality to the
muted shades •

Carpet moss
A good material
for cladding •

Silver reindeer moss •
Pin a mossy grass verge at the hedge base

HEDGEROW WITH TREE

Dreaming up excitingly new, different things to do with plants is a satisfying aspect of working with such versatile materials. For this wall hanging, I took some familiar dried ingredients, added basic DIY skills and equipment (a handful of screws; a screwdriver; a heavy-duty staple gun), and created a picture that will last for months and is easily adapted to your own design. Not a bit out of place in this English country setting, the terracotta figures are by Mrs. Brown, from the island of Nevis in the West Indies.

You'll find detailed instructions for making this dried flower picture on pages 44 and 45.

Lily Wedding Circlets

Choosing the colours for wedding bouquets and headdresses can be a taxing matter, as fashions change from pastels to primaries to tones of a single colour. You have only to look at great paintings, or indeed great gardens, to see how well many different colour combinations can work, both likely and unlikely ones. But the fashion for cream or ivory bridal dresses seems to endure, and this is fortunate, for with a dress in this colour range, almost any flowers will look just right. In these circlets for a bride and young bridesmaid, soft pink and coral blend with yellow, and are set off by hues of green. Don't forget a blue flower, for good luck, in the bride's circlet.

What you will need

For the bride's circlet
- *Stout stub wires, joined to head circumference plus 2cm (¾in)*
- *Gutta percha tape*
- *Fine reel wire*
- *5 stems berried ruscus*
- *6 houttuynia leaves*
- *5 stems yellow alstroemeria*
- *5 stems pink & white lisianthus*
- *1 borage flower*

For the bridesmaid's circlet
- *Ready-made twisted stem circle*
- *Glue gun*
- *5 trails creeping Jenny*
- *6 houttuynia leaves*
- *5 stems yellow roses*
- *3 stems coral Guernsey lilies*

How to make them

The bride's circlet is made on a Flexible Base *(see pages 24–25).* Bind the stub-wire base with tape, and form a round eye at one end. Attach mixed bunches of leaves and flowers to the base with reel wire. Bind the reel wire with tape before attaching the next bunch. Secure the end through the eye. For the bridesmaid, simply glue the flowers onto the stem circle.

Guernsey lily •
The frilly petals of this nerine variety curl back to reveal slender stamens of the same colour

• **Twisted stem circle**
The bridesmaid's circlet is made on a base of intertwined vines

Creeping Jenny •
Trails of tiny leaves add accents of pale greeny gold

Yellow rose •
Rosa 'Landia' has small flowers and a wonderful perfume

Borage
Signifying courage, this herb has delicate, star-shaped blue flowers

Ruscus
Choose stems with berries on them, if possible

Houttuynia 'Chamaeleon'
When crushed, the leaves release the pungent scent of bitter oranges

Alstroemeria
These flowers last well out of water, so are ideal for a bridal circlet

Lisianthus
Use a mix of open flowers with pastel-edged petals, and pure white buds

49

WHEATFIELD BUNDLES

IT IS EASY TO FORGET just how beautiful wheat-sheaves can look, particularly now that they are no longer a commonplace sight, standing, regimented, in newly harvested fields. These two arrangements are quite simple to make, as they are really nothing more complicated than large bundles of stalks that fan out above and below a tie. On a small scale, and with the addition of a few dried flowers that look as if they could be growing wild in a wheatfield, they make an informal but still extremely picturesque wall hanging. The plaited raffia ties that go around the bundles complement the natural feel of the plant material.

WHAT YOU WILL NEED

FOR THE SMALL BUNDLE
• *Twine, for tying*
• *Mossing wire*
• *2cm (¾in) thick bunch natural raffia, 1m (39in) long*
• *Few extra natural raffia strands, for tying plait*
• *160 stalks cone wheat*
• *7 stems yellow cluster-flowered everlasting*
• *10 stems red miniature spray roses*

FOR THE LARGE BUNDLE
• *Twine, for tying*
• *Mossing wire*
• *4cm (1½in) thick bunch natural raffia, 1.25m (49in) long*
• *Few extra natural raffia strands, for tying plait*
• *400 stalks cone wheat*
• *15 love-in-a-mist seedheads*
• *7 stems blue delphinium*
• *10 stems red miniature spray roses*

Cluster-flowered everlasting
Helichrysum italicum *is a variety of strawflower that has numerous small heads of woolly blooms*

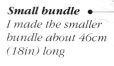

Small bundle
I made the smaller bundle about 46cm (18in) long

HOW TO MAKE THEM

The two bundles are made in the same way. Make the raffia bunch into a thin plait. Bunch together a large handful of wheatstalks, with the heads layered down the sides a little, adding a few flower sprigs as you go. Tie three times: below the ears; in the middle; and 10cm (4in) from the bottom. Now layer in more wheat and flowers, tying in their stems about two-thirds of the way down. Fan out the stems at the bottom and cut level. Tie a plait in a bow around the bundle. Secure its centre with a raffia tie.

Plaited raffia bow
Stop the bow coming undone by tying its centre with mossing wire before you add the raffia tie

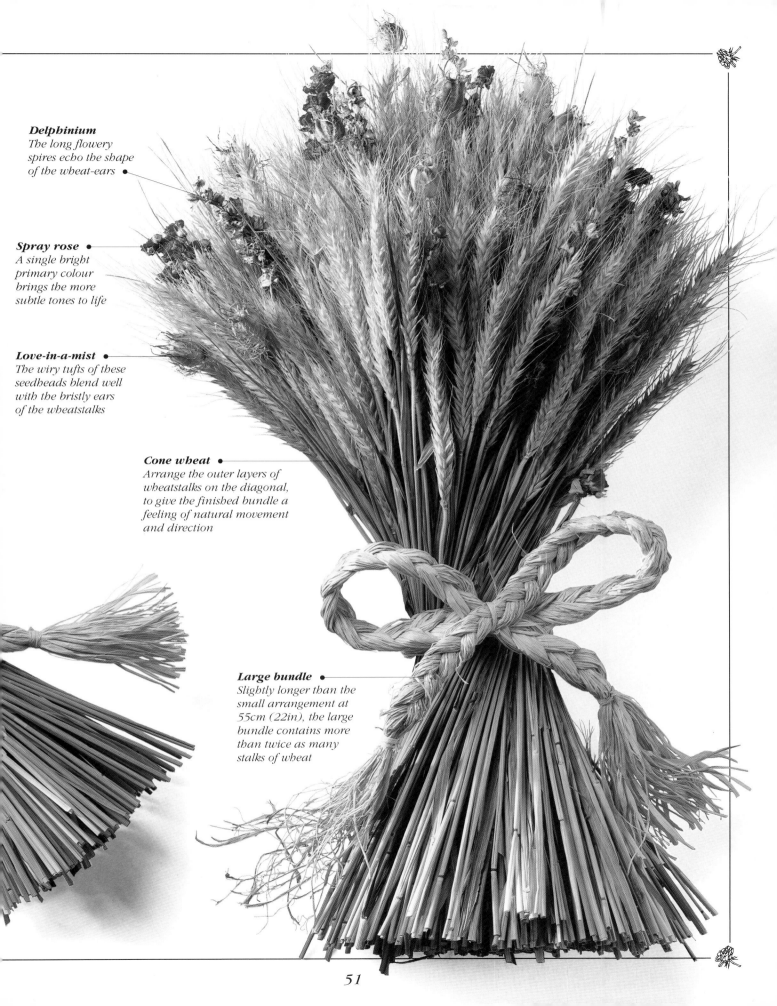

Delphinium
The long flowery
spires echo the shape
of the wheat-ears

Spray rose
A single bright
primary colour
brings the more
subtle tones to life

Love-in-a-mist
The wiry tufts of these
seedheads blend well
with the bristly ears
of the wheatstalks

Cone wheat
Arrange the outer layers of
wheatstalks on the diagonal,
to give the finished bundle a
feeling of natural movement
and direction

Large bundle
Slightly longer than the
small arrangement at
55cm (22in), the large
bundle contains more
than twice as many
stalks of wheat

CANDY STRIPE GARLAND

COLOURS AND TEXTURES are all-important when you are planning fresh flower garlands for a grand occasion. Because garlands often have to compete with an array of other visual delights (and especially if they are to be seen by and through a host of people, maybe at a wedding or big party), I like to choose a combination of delicate as well as bold flowers and leaves for them. Here, small bunches of stripy pink and white flowers – sweet-scented roses and carnations, pink-veined salvia, and single alstroemeria – stand out colourfully against the dense, feathery foliage of tree asparagus, wispy green heads of love-in-a-mist, and silvery eucalyptus discs.

WHAT YOU WILL NEED

FOR EVERY 1M (39IN) OF GARLAND

- *1m (39in) stout cord*
- *Medium-gauge stub wires*
- *Reel wire*
- *5 stems pink & white alstroemeria flowers*
- *12 pink & white zebra roses*
- *10 pink & white carnations*
- *5 stems green love-in-a-mist*
- *6 stems* Salvia horminum
- *8 stems silver gum eucalyptus*
- *12 stems tree asparagus*

HOW TO MAKE IT

This dainty garland is made on a FLEXIBLE BASE *(see pages 24–25)*. Start off by wiring single flowers of the alstroemeria *(see page 22)*, and the roses and carnations *(see page 23)*. Make up small, mixed bunches of all the wired flowers, including sprigs of love-in-a-mist, salvia, eucalyptus, and plenty of tree asparagus in each one. Bind each bunch to the base cord with reel wire as you make it, so that its head overlaps the stems of the previous bunch. Fill in gaps with any remaining flowers and leaves.

Silver gum
This eucalyptus species has oval leaves of a beautiful dusky blue

Tree asparagus
The spires of feathery foliage are perfect for filling out garlands

Love-in-a-mist
Choose a variety
with green flowers,
as I have, or one in
blue or white

Salvia horminum
Pale pink bracts,
veined in a deeper
hue, surround the
tiny flowers

Zebra rose
Crushed raspberry
pink stripes mottle
the petals of this
unusual cultivar

Carnation
The scent of cloves
gives these flowers
a spicy fragrance

Alstroemeria
Spots and stripes
provide delicate
splashes of colour

LARKSPUR RAFFIA RING

A SIMPLE AND HOMELY LOOKING ring made of dried country flowers and seedcases is just right for hanging against the natural wood of an unpainted door, or on one of the walls of an enclosed porchway, where it will be protected from the weather. The base of this wreath is a thick raffia plait, joined into a circle. A decorative, thinner plaited bow covers the join of the two ends. To blend with the biscuity tones of the raffia, I've chosen strawflowers of a somewhat paler colour, together with larkspur in two subtle shades of blue, spiky grey-blue globe thistle heads, and fronds of pale green miniature honesty. The flowers spray out from the ring of plaited raffia in an exuberant swirl, like sparks flying from a spinning Catherine wheel.

WHAT YOU WILL NEED

- *1 thick bunch natural raffia, 1.5m (59in) long*
- *1 thin bunch natural raffia, 75cm (30in) long*
- *Medium-gauge stub wires*
- *25 stems lavender-blue larkspur*
- *25 stems navy-blue larkspur*
- *25 stems ivory strawflowers*
- *45 sprigs miniature honesty seedcase fronds*
- *20 heads miniature globe thistle*

HOW TO MAKE IT

This large wreath is made on a RIGID BASE *(see page 27, MAKING A PLAITED RAFFIA RING)*.
The base for this circle needs to be quite substantial, so that it will hold its shape without drooping when the flowers are in and the wreath is hung up. Use the long raffia bunch to make a plait 6cm (2½in) thick. Join the ends to form a circle 38cm (15in) in diameter.

Miniature honesty •
Arrange the seedcase fronds with the flowers so that they hang free around the ring in a clockwise direction

Larkspur •
This lovely cottage-garden plant dries extremely well, and you can grow dwarf forms in containers if you have no garden

Make a narrow plait with the thin bunch of raffia and tie into a bow. Bind the bow over the join of the circle with a raffia strand or two. Set aside a few stems of larkspur. Make up small bunches of all the remaining plant material *(see page 22)*. Push the wire of each bunch into the plait, securing and hiding it inside the raffia strands. Fill any gaps with the remaining larkspur.

The finished ring
Hung out of bright light, this dried
flower arrangement will last and
look good for many months

Miniature globe thistle
The spiky round heads make a
nice visual contrast with the
flowing larkspur spires and
fronds of miniature honesty

Strawflower
A soft shade of white
brightens the deeper
colours, but doesn't
jar against them

EXOTIC WALL BASKET

FINDING THE IDEAL PLACE to display arrangements of flowers for special occasions is not always easy. Side tables must be cleared away to make standing room for guests, and all the space on the dining table is often taken up with food. Wall baskets solve dilemmas of this kind, as they can be hung up on the wall like paintings, anywhere you like. The exotic *mélange* of flowers that fills this wire vegetable half-basket includes the highly scented tuberose. Its pervasive, spicily sweet fragrance will fill the largest of rooms within moments.

WHAT YOU WILL NEED

- *25cm (10in) diameter wire mesh half-basket*
- *3 double handfuls damp sphagnum or carpet moss*
- *Stout plastic garden trash bag*
- *3 bricks wet foam, well soaked*
- *9 stems tuberose*
- *5 stems gloriosa lilies*
- *3 stems green anthurium*
- *1 stem deep yellow Cymbidium orchids*
- *10 stems greeny-yellow miniature Singapore orchids*
- *3 stems pink miniature Singapore orchids*
- *3 stems mahonia leaves*
- *5 stems purplish leucadendron*
- *5 large poplar or other leaves*

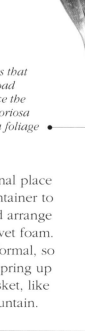

Gloriosa lily foliage
This climbing plant uses the ends of its leaves as tendrils

Poplar leaf
Choose any leaves that are large and broad enough to balance the linearity of the gloriosa lily and mahonia foliage

HOW TO MAKE IT

Use any sort of half-basket that is suitable to plant up and hang on an outside wall. For a wire mesh basket, first line all except its flat back with damp moss. Then line the entire basket with plastic. Cut pieces of soaked wet foam to fill the pocket: make them fit snugly.

Hang your basket in its final place (or stand it in another container to hold it firmly upright) and arrange the plant material in the wet foam. Keep the arrangement informal, so that the flowers seem to spring up from the centre of the basket, like water gushing out of a fountain.

Tuberose
Use with caution, as
the deep scent is not
always welcome

Miniature orchid
For longer-lasting blooms,
stand the orchid stems in
deep water for some hours
before you make the basket

Anthurium
A green form of these
usually red, odd
flowers adds a
novel touch

Leucadendron
These leathery leaves
are produced by an
evergreen shrub

Cymbidium orchid
You can get this "queen of
exotic flowers" in almost
every colour except blue

Gloriosa lily flower
The wavy-edged petals
and dancing stamens
make the flowers look
especially graceful

Mahonia leaf
Each leaflet lobe ends in a vicious spike,
so be careful how you handle these leaves

INGENIOUS WIRE RING

UNDERSTATED ELEGANCE AND SIMPLICITY are the hallmarks of this copper and gold circular garland, which looks equally good in formal and informal settings. Find a plain-coloured wall to display it against, though, for as with most unframed wall-hangings, it would get lost against a very busy wallpaper. To my mind, this garland has the appearance of something at once ancient and precious, so would suit a cool, contemporary location particularly. When acorns are in season, I would gild and add just a few, to enhance the oak leaves. One note of caution: if your household includes cats, don't hang the garland any place within their reach, for feathers are like ambrosia to cats, and they could easily destroy your creation in moments.

WHAT YOU WILL NEED

- *1m (39in) lightweight electrical copper-wire cable*
- *1m (39in) heavy-duty electrical copper-wire cable*
- *Gold spray paint*
- *Strong multi-purpose glue*
- *25 pressed oak or beech leaves*
- *10 duck or other feathers*

Copper-wire tendril •
When coiling the wire for the tendrils, wind it very tightly around the pencil, but extend each coil more or less to get tendrils of a varying springiness

Duck feather •
I got these free from my local friendly fishmonger, but you could use any feathers that suit the restrained tone of the other ingredients in the ring

HOW TO MAKE IT

Start by stripping away the casing of the lightweight electrical cable. Separate the copper wires inside and lay them straight. Strip off the casing of the heavy-duty wire, but unwind the wires gently to keep their wavy curves intact. Spray the oak leaves with gold paint. Make the nine curly tendrils by winding 30cm (12in) lengths of the finer wire around a thin round pencil. Leave a straight end of 5cm (2in), and extend the spiral slightly as you pull each of the tendrils off the pencil. Loosely bend five of the heavy wires into a ring 38cm (15in) in diameter, so that their ends just overlap. Weave in three more wires to form the three free ends. Use the finer wire to tie off any joins. Bind the tendrils to the ring by their straight ends. Lastly, attach the leaves and feathers in position with spots of strong glue.

Gilded leaf
Spray the leaves a rich gold
on the top side only, letting
the natural leaf colour show
through in some places as I
did, or on both sides

Copper-wire free end
Where leaves and feathers
are glued on, don't try to
hide any joins – just see
the leaf stems as part of
the decoration

Pressed oak leaf
Look out for leaves on
countryside rambles
or walks in the park,
then press them – at
home – between two
books to dry out

59

JAUNTY GARLAND

MOSTLY, I LIKE TO USE FLOWERS in their own growing season, but there are times, particularly in the middle of winter, when it's comforting to know that year-round varieties are still available in a broad range of colours. With its combination of seasonless flowers, this vivid garland could be made at almost any time of year. Gerberas, roses, and orchids all come in a host of colours that will allow you to match the mood of your garland to its location. My zingy orange and pink scheme is continued in the jaunty starfish and spirals of rich pink ribbon. Balance the strength of the other colours with leaves in a bold green.

Mexican orange blossom
The foliage of this evergreen shrub is sweetly aromatic

Dried starfish •
Use an electric drill at slow speed (or a hand drill) fitted with a fine bit to make tiny holes in the starfish for the gold hanging-threads

Galax •
With their uncomplicated shape, strong colour, and fine network of veining, galax leaves provide the perfect background and foil for the flowers

Miniature orchid •
Finding flowers so like the starfish was a stroke of luck!

WHAT YOU WILL NEED

FOR EVERY 1M (39IN) OF GARLAND
- *1m (39in) stout cord*
- *Medium-gauge stub wires*
- *Reel wire*
- *12 pink gerbera flowers*
- *5 peach-pink roses*
- *5 lime-green single orchids*
- *5 stems each orange & deep pink miniature Singapore orchids*
- *20 galax leaves*
- *15 sprigs variegated ivy*
- *10 sprigs Mexican orange blossom foliage*
- *10 orange dried starfish, strung with metallic gold thread*
- *3m (10ft) shocking pink wire-edged ribbon, 4cm (1½in) wide*

HOW TO MAKE IT

This garland is made on a FLEXIBLE BASE *(see pages 24–25)*.
Start by wiring short stems of the gerbera flowers, the roses, and all the orchids *(see page 23)*. Make up small bunches of these wired flowers, together with pieces of all the foliage. Bind each bunch to the cord with reel wire as you make it, so that its head overlaps the stalks of the previous bunch.

If the garland is to hang against a table *(see pages 62–63)*, use fine tacks to secure it to the top edge in scallops. Fasten the scallops to the cloth with safety pins pushed through from back to front. Fill in with extra flowers to beautify the garland, then hang the starfish by their gold threads. Spiral ribbon through, and fix a multi-looped bow at the apex of each scallop.

Single orchid
Lime-green adds unexpected visual accents to my flower theme of pink and orange

Variegated ivy
Clumps of creamy foliage stop the garland looking too dense and heavy

Gerbera
Equally versatile for special and everyday arrangements, these daisy-like flowers are available throughout the year as large or miniature blooms, in a choice of jolly, vivacious colours

Rose
Choose small, tight buds that will open out in the heat of a warm room

JAUNTY GARLAND

*Weddings and anniversaries;
a college graduation; the
birth of a child: the lives of
our families and bosom
friends are punctuated with
landmark events that seem as
if tailor made for celebrating
in exuberant style. Add a
touch of magic to the
occasion, and make it one
always to remember, by
garlanding not just serving
tables, but window- and
door-frames too, with
sumptuously ribbon-decked
festoons of dazzling fresh
flowers and brilliant foliage.*

You'll find detailed instructions
for making this fresh flower
garland on pages 60 and 61.

MARIGOLD HEART

WHAT COULD BE MORE WELCOMING for an anniversary or birthday celebration in high summer than a simple heart of flowers hanging on the front door, where it will be seen by each one of your guests the minute they arrive. If you have a garden, then this is the time of year when it's ablaze with flowers that echo the colours and feel of sunshine and unclouded skies; and summer is especially the season to enjoy sweet cottagey flowers, like the delphiniums and pot marigolds that I've used in my heart-shaped wreath. Don't be fearful of combining flowers with jazzily contrasting colours: just pack them close together to your own design, and let them work their wonders.

WHAT YOU WILL NEED

- *43cm (17in) diameter heart-shaped wet foam wreath base*
- *60 tips* Euonymus fortunei *'Emerald and Gold'*
- *20 stems pot marigolds*
- *20 heads red globe amaranth*
- *20 stems* Chrysanthemum carinatum *'Monarch Court Jesters'*
- *2 stems blue delphinium*
- *2m (6½ft) pink & white wire-edged ribbon, 3cm (1¼in) wide*

HOW TO MAKE IT

Soak the wet foam wreath base in water until the foam has taken up enough water to be damp all the way through. Do not oversoak it, though, or the base will be heavy and also drip when it is hung up. Cut all of the foliage and flowers, except the delphinium stems, into pieces 7.5cm (3in) long. Separate the delphinium stems into florets.

Globe amaranth
The dense, clover-like heads of flowers are produced from summer through to the early autumn, and keep their rich colours – red, orange, purple, pink, or white – when dried •

First, put in the tips of variegated euonymus. Arrange the foliage at an angle, and running in a single direction around the heart. Put in the marigolds next, spacing them unevenly, but keeping a balanced feel to the arrangement. Now put in some clusters as well as single heads of globe amaranth flowers. Place the chrysanthemums, again keeping a good balance between the different colour tones. Finally, tuck florets of blue delphinium in among the other flowers. Cut the ribbon into short lengths of about 15cm (6in) or so, and spiral them in around the flowers and foliage.

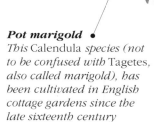

Pot marigold •
This Calendula *species (not to be confused with* Tagetes, *also called marigold), has been cultivated in English cottage gardens since the late sixteenth century*

Euonymus
Use foliage with a golden
variegation that picks up
the brilliant yellow of the
chrysanthemum and pot
• marigold flowers

Chrysanthemum
Look again if you think
chrysanthemum means
autumnal oranges and
browns: each daisy head
of 'Monarch Court Jesters'
sports three lively colours
and a starburst centre

Delphinium
I chose the intensely coloured
'Blue Bee' so that the single
florets – though small and
delicate – really sing out

Lots of Pods

Some seeds and pods have fascinating shapes that can be used to cunning advantage in many sorts of arrangements. This wall-mounted plaque has something about it that calls to mind an armorial shield. It combines clusters of tropical seedheads and pods, arranged in a random yet symmetrical oval pattern, with bundles of wheat. A rich blue and gold Napoleonic silk ribbon binds the stalks of wheat, and forms a decorative cockade at the intersection of the bundles. With such an ornate ribbon, this creation would do justice to a formal dining or sitting room. A simpler ribbon, perhaps a tartan one, is a better choice for casual settings.

Wheatstalks •
The smooth, not whiskery, ears of bread wheat suit the clean lines and firm forms of this bold design

Tropical seedpod
Look out for exotic varieties like this where dried flowers are the speciality, and also in some home design shops •

Tropical seedhead
Buy as great a selection of shapes and textures as you can get hold of •

What you will need

- *1 piece chicken wire, 75cm (30in) long & 30cm (12in) wide*
- *9 handfuls dry sphagnum moss*
- *Medium-gauge stub wires, some bent as hairpins 10cm (4in) long*
- *Reel wire*
- *Glue gun*
- *4 large handfuls natural undyed Spanish moss*
- *80 wheatstalks*
- *50–60 assorted tropical dried seedheads & pods*
- *5 large dried mushroom cones*
- *2m (6½ft) wire-edged silk or other ribbon, 5cm (2in) wide*

How to make it

This wall hanging is made on a Mattress Base *(see pages 30–31)*. Make an oval mattress of moss-filled chicken wire. Place a layer of moss on one half of the piece of chicken wire. Make it as wide as the chicken wire, 38cm (15in) long, and 2.5cm (1in) or so thick. Fold the other half of the piece of chicken wire lengthways over the moss, then fold in the corners to form an oval. Cover with Spanish moss, attached with wire hairpins. Gather the wheat into two even-sized bundles, grading the heads downwards. Cut two 30cm (12in) lengths of ribbon and bind one around each bundle, spiralling it down the stalks. Secure behind, then attach to the mattress, using wire hairpins. Wire the seedheads and pods *(see page 22)*. Poke the wires through to the back of the mattress and secure. Glue on the mushrooms. Wire a multiple bow at the centre of the arrangement.

Dried mushroom
The cones are thin
• *and very fragile*

• **Spanish moss**
Cladding the base with moss
gives the edges an attractive
finish, and ensures that no
patches of chicken wire are
visible in the arrangement

AUTUMN BRIDAL RING

THE MUTED FLOWERS OF HYDRANGEA and globe amaranth, and the fluffy seedheads of wild clematis, encircle a twig frame of willow canes in this mellow wreath. A charming alternative to the more usual bridal bouquet, the ring is light and easy to carry on the day, and can be dried afterwards to make a sweet keepsake. This adventurous creation, which would be lovely for a wedding in the autumn, looks very special against an ivory and gold dress. Complete the bridal picture with a twig headdress, and miniature rings of the same flowers for the bridesmaids to carry.

WHAT YOU WILL NEED

- *10 thin willow canes, 1.5m (59in) long*
- *Glue gun*
- *30 small hydrangea florets, in mixed pinks, blues, & greens*
- *30 globe amaranth flowers, in shades of warm pink & coral*
- *8 long trails wild clematis*
- *2m (6½ft) blue & gold silk ribbon, 4cm (1½in) wide*

Hydrangea •
Use a domed, mop-headed variety, which will furnish you with a very generous number of small florets from each large flower

HOW TO MAKE IT

Entwine the supple willow canes, joining the ends to make a circle 30cm (12in) in diameter. Glue all the hydrangea florets and globe amaranth flowers onto the circle, leaving a space at the top to form the handle. Cut the wild clematis trails into short lengths. Use small dabs of glue to attach them here and there among the flowers. Fill in the plant material on one side, with the ring lying flat, then hang it up and fill in the back, for both sides will be on display. Bind the top space with ribbon, and attach flowing ribbon tails to the handle.

Silk ribbon tails •
Ideally, your choice of ribbon should be as extravagant as the budget allows: gorgeous ribbon like mine won't be a bargain, but any important event is worth some expense

Covered handle
Ribbon wound around
this part of the entwined
willow-cane base provides
a decorative finish and a
more comfortable handle

Globe amaranth
You may need to hunt a bit
for these striking shades of
warm pink, as they're less
easy to come by than the
clear, bright colours •

Wild clematis
Lovely country names for this
plant are old man's beard or
traveller's joy, evoking a long
life with moments of rapture
for one partner (at least) of
the new-married twosome

RUSTIC BUNCHES

SIMPLE CREATIONS ARE EVERY BIT as effective as the more elaborate arrangements, and you can make a pretty decoration for your home just by hanging bunches of dried flowers against a wall or on a door. Your own choice of colour scheme for the flowers and foliage should work well with the place in which the bunches will hang, but need not be a slavish match to the surroundings. The two bunches that I've put together here both use the silvery foliage of artemisia, but with different flowers in the same colour range of peach, orange, and red, each has a unique and special charm. Finish the bunches with rustic ribbons, and hang them out of strong sunlight.

WHAT YOU WILL NEED

FOR THE SMALL BUNCH
- *Twine, for tying*
- *10 stems artemisia foliage*
- *15 stems red roses*
- *15 stems orange strawflowers*
- *10 heads safflower*
- *1m (39in) grey-green grosgrain ribbon, 4cm (1½in) wide*

FOR THE LARGE BUNCH
- *Twine, for tying*
- *10 stems artemisia foliage*
- *25 stems peach-pink roses*
- *20 stems red bottlebrush*
- *1m (39in) peach-pink grosgrain ribbon, 4cm (1½in) wide*

HOW TO MAKE THEM

These bunches are both made in the same very easy way. Start off by putting together a narrow fan of the longest stems of artemisia foliage, roses, strawflowers, and safflower heads (or bottlebrush). This fixes the shape of the bunch. Now layer in the remaining plant material, making sure that there are flowers and foliage almost as far as the point at which the bow will be attached. Bind the bunch firmly around with twine, tying it 10cm (4in) or so from the ends of the stems. Cut 30cm (12in) from the length of ribbon. Tie the rest into a double bow, and attach to the bunch with the short length.

Strawflower
This well-known everlasting is popular everywhere; easy to find in almost any place that sells dried flowers; and usually good value besides

Rose
Even when dried, deeply scented varieties retain a vestige of fragrance that reminds us of their sweet, full-blown summer glory

Safflower
The tufty, thistle-like heads of safflower yield a bright orange-yellow dye, giving the plant its traditional name of dyer's saffron

Uneven stems
I think the informality of a not-too-even finish is quite charming, but you could cut the stem ends level if you're keen on neatness

Ribbon bow with tails
The closely ribbed weave of grosgrain ribbon suits the rough textures of the dried plant ingredients

Bottlebrush
Native to all parts of Australia, the many species of bottlebrush have insignificant flowers, but myriad colourful and slender stamens, which surround the stem in clusters of soft spikes

Artemisia
Use these feathery stems of pleasantly aromatic, grey-green foliage as a single, unifying theme that flows through the two separate bunches

GALA SWAG

Globe artichoke
*The tight-closed buds
have a sculptural look
that contrasts sharply
with the magnificent
open flowerheads*

Heather
*Trailing bunches of bell
heather encourage the
naturally downward
direction of the swag*

COLOUR PLAYS A CONSIDERABLE PART in our everyday lives. It
conjures atmospheres, affects our mood, and provides us
with all manner of associations. This gloriously rich swag
would be a wonderful decoration for an autumn wedding
party. Even though there is something about the mood of
its colour scheme that reminds me instantly of autumn, the
swag doesn't contain the colours that are usually associated
with that time of year – those dusky rusts, reds, and oranges
that I think are a little sombre for such a joyous occasion as a
wedding. Rather, it combines a toothsome range of pinks that
runs from the deep lilac-pink of the globe artichoke flowers to
the orange-pink of the celosia. Pink-budded viburnum strikes a
vibrant chord, and clumps of heather bring abundant good luck.

Viburnum
*In autumn, this evergreen shrub
(also called laurustinus) offers
you a quartet of delights: glossy
green leaves; pink buds; white
flowers; and blue berry-fruits
shaped as tiny ovals* •

• **Celosia cockscomb**
*Despite its exotic appearance,
this plant is no bother to grow,
and the squiggly, soft, almost
irresistibly touchable flower
plumes add richness to any
arrangement at a stroke*

WHAT YOU WILL NEED

- *1 piece chicken wire, 165cm
(65in) long & 20cm (8in) wide*
- *20 handfuls sphagnum moss*
- *Medium-gauge stub wires*
- *Reel wire*
- *30 sprigs deep pink heather*
- *12 globe artichoke flowers*
- *10 stems celosia cockscomb,
in shades of pink & orange-pink*
- *60 sprigs viburnum foliage
with flowers, some in bud*

HOW TO MAKE IT

This swag is made on a RIGID BASE
(see page 26, MAKING A CIRCULAR
CHICKEN WIRE AND MOSS BASE).
Roll the chicken wire around the
moss to form the base. Bend into
shape. Wire heather in bunches,
artichoke flowers, and pieces of
celosia *(see page 22)*. Leave each
with a 15cm (6in) stub-wire end.
Push sprigs of viburnum into the
base to cover its front, then wire
in the flowers. Give everything a
fluid movement down to the base
of the loop and the two tail ends.

THE EPITOME OF SUMMER

EARLY SUMMER IS A MAGICAL TIME of the year – the time when most of our favourite flowers are in their prime. Peonies, sweet peas, roses, lilies, ranunculus, delphiniums: of all flowers, these are among the most sumptuous, and not only for their looks, as many are also lusciously scented. This ring epitomizes the mood of summer perfectly, its shades of pink set off by golden-green foliage and glints of sharp yellow. Here are great fat peonies, their sweet scent and cupped petals mixing with the spicy fragrance and calm beauty of the lily trumpets. Spires of deep red orchids and peachily pink ranunculus, like miniature peonies, appear among these more showy flowers, with deft touches of yellow kangaroo paw that enliven the softer colours. For a summer treat, invite favoured friends to dine outside, and set this lovely ring close to the table.

Vanda orchid •
Arrange the spires so that some longer stems with buds are mingled among shorter clusters of full-blown blossoms

WHAT YOU WILL NEED

- *30cm (12in) diameter circular wet foam wreath base*
- *5 stems eucalyptus foliage*
- *8 pink peonies*
- *10 white & pink oriental lilies*
- *10 stems pink ranunculus*
- *10 stems deep burgundy-red Vanda orchids*
- *3 stems yellow kangaroo paw*

Kangaroo paw •
The white flowers of this native Australian plant are completely enclosed at first by their slender, felted yellow sepals

HOW TO MAKE IT

You can buy wet foam bases in good flower shops and in many garden centres. Begin by soaking the base according to the maker's instructions. The foam should be damp through. Do not oversoak it, or the base will be very heavy and also drip when it is hung up. Arrange the plant material clockwise above the centre of the ring

and anticlockwise below it. Put in sprigs of eucalyptus foliage first, then place the peonies, disposing them in a random fashion. As lily pollen stains, remove the stamens before arranging the flowers into the ring. Put groups of ranunculus at both the outer and inner edges, interspersed with pieces of orchid and a sprinkle of kangaroo paw.

Eucalyptus •
Unless you specially like its pungent scent, choose young foliage that is not too aromatic; or go for the species known as lemon-scented gum

Ranunculus
This flower belongs to
the same plant family
as the lowly buttercup
and ethereal peony

Peony
I love these gorgeous,
silken-petalled blooms,
and their brief season
makes them seem even
more precious

Oriental lily
The creamy flutes
of Lilium 'Pompeii'
reveal dainty pink
markings as they
unfold and open

MELLOW HOP SWAG

AUTUMN ARRIVES, AND ONCE MORE the colour spectrum changes, from the clear, bright tones of summer to the warm baked-earth colours of the setting sun and of smoky bonfires. Embrace this transition into the new season, and celebrate the good feel of autumn, with a garland of dried hop flowers, yarrow, golden strawflowers, rusty cress seedheads, and ruby chillies, all intertwined with loops of tawny paper ribbon. The green of the hops highlights the duskier hues, making the whole garland glow.

WHAT YOU WILL NEED

FOR EVERY 1M (39IN) OF GARLAND
- *1m (39in) stout cord*
- *Reel wire*
- *6 bunches cress seedheads*
- *15 sprigs hop flowers*
- *6 stems yarrow*
- *20 stems yellow strawflowers*
- *15 red preserved chillies*
- *2m (6½ft) coiled paper ribbon*

HOW TO MAKE IT

This chunky garland is made on a FLEXIBLE BASE *(see pages 24–25).* Cut the paper ribbon into 30cm (12in) lengths, and fan them out. Make up bunches of all the plant material, wiring in the chillies and loops of ribbon as you go. Bind the bunches to the cord with reel wire as you make them, attaching the few back stems of each bunch to those of the bunch it overlaps. This keeps the garland together, and makes it easier to hang. Add some extra flowers and ribbon loops once it's hung in place.

Cress
These airy fronds, which vary in tone from greenish brown through to russet red, have a pleasantly crunchy feel and texture that creates a perfect background for the other plant ingredients

Yarrow
'Coronation Gold' *is a cultivar of the species* Achillea filipendulina, *which has an exceptional colour and dries well*

Strawflower
Choose heads of the deepest gold that you can find

Preserved chilli
These can sting skin as much as fresh ones, so wash your hands after handling them

Hop
Only female plants produce these drooping clusters of cone-like flower bracts

Paper ribbon
The compact coils look a bit unpromising, but are easy to stretch out

MELLOW HOP SWAG

*Everyone has a favourite
season, and if autumn is
yours, I feel sure you'll love
the evocative, bittersweet
colour palette of this quickly
made swag. Its deep reds and
golden yellows recall the
shimmering heat of summer;
bronze seedheads tell of bare
winter earth; but the fragile
green hop flowers remind us
that spring will follow on.
Drape your swag around a
log-filled fireplace, or twine it
down a staircase, as I did:
either way, it'll look glorious.*

You'll find detailed instructions
for making this dried flower
swag on pages 76 and 77.

HOT CHILLI BONANZA

HANG THIS TWISTED STEM CIRCLE of pods, berries, and flowers on your front door as a brilliant beacon to greet a group of close friends arriving at an autumn harvest thanksgiving party. You can be sure that the festivities will get off to a lively start. All of the plant material that I've put together for this wreath is fresh, except for the orange safflower heads, and will last well. Even when the chilli peppers and strands of privet and celastrus berries have shrivelled, the circle will still have an attractively faded appeal. The colour range brings to this arrangement all the rich tones of autumn, through yellow to orange, red, and inky black; and, of course, autumn is the prime time for finding the ingredients.

WHAT YOU WILL NEED

- *55cm (22in) diameter ready-made twisted stem circle or*
- *10 thin willow or hazel canes, 1.5m (59in) long*
- *Mossing wire*
- *Glue gun*
- *3 stems each green, yellow, & red chillies*
- *5 stems round orange chillies*
- *3 stems berried privet*
- *5 stems berried celastrus*
- *30 heads dried safflower*

Celastrus •
This twining climber is grown especially for its beautiful red and yellow fruits

Privet •
Arrange the glossy black berries in small clusters and some larger clumps around the circle

HOW TO MAKE IT

You can buy twig or stem wreath bases similar to the one I've used here in most good flower shops and many garden centres. Or you could try making one yourself. To do this, take four or five of the willow or hazel canes. Twist and bend them together into a circle roughly 55cm (22in) in diameter. Overlap the ends and secure with mossing wire. Build up additional layers with the remaining canes.

Secure them into the twisted base layer by threading and spiralling them through the existing canes. Trim all the plant material so that each piece measures 15cm (6in) long or so. Tuck the chillies into the base first, wedging their stalks firmly in between the overlapping canes. Add the strands of privet and celastrus berries and, lastly, the safflowers. Glue on any short pieces that cannot be wedged in.

Serrano chilli •
Choose stems of these very hot red chilli peppers with a few unripe green pods

Cascabel chilli
This variety gets its name from
a Spanish word for rattle

Safflower
The strange thistle-like heads
retain their wonderfully sunny
orange-gold colour when dried

Jalapeño pepper
Originally from Mexico,
these fiery chillies are
also good pickled

Szechuan chilli
The elegant yellow pods
are edible, as are all the
chillies that decorate
this twisted stem circle

WINTER-WHITE SWAG

Euonymus
The deciduous Euonymus
europaeus *'Red Cascade'
will give you radiant red
berries with orange seeds
bunched on leafless twigs*

Strawflower
*The bare silver birch twigs
demand decoration that's
equally unassuming, like
these modest dried blooms*

LOVELY IN ITS SPARE AUSTERITY, this twiggy dried swag seems to me
to encapsulate all the grey beauty of winter. The shape of the
swag is fashioned from four slender bundles of silver birch
twigs. Two bundles face from either side into the middle
to form the central loop, while the two others make the
hanging sides. I've used mostly dried flowers in shades
of white to dress the twigs: creamy strawflowers; heads
of pearly everlasting in tufty clumps; and ivory peonies
that retain the sweetness of their early summer perfume
many months after the blooms have been gathered and
dried. Woven among the flowers, tiny euonymus berries
flash inspiring sparks of Chinese red. The looped bows of
silky, grey grosgrain ribbon add a quiet flourish. This swag
would make a simple yet graceful decoration for a fireplace,
or you might use it to frame a kitchen dresser-top or window.

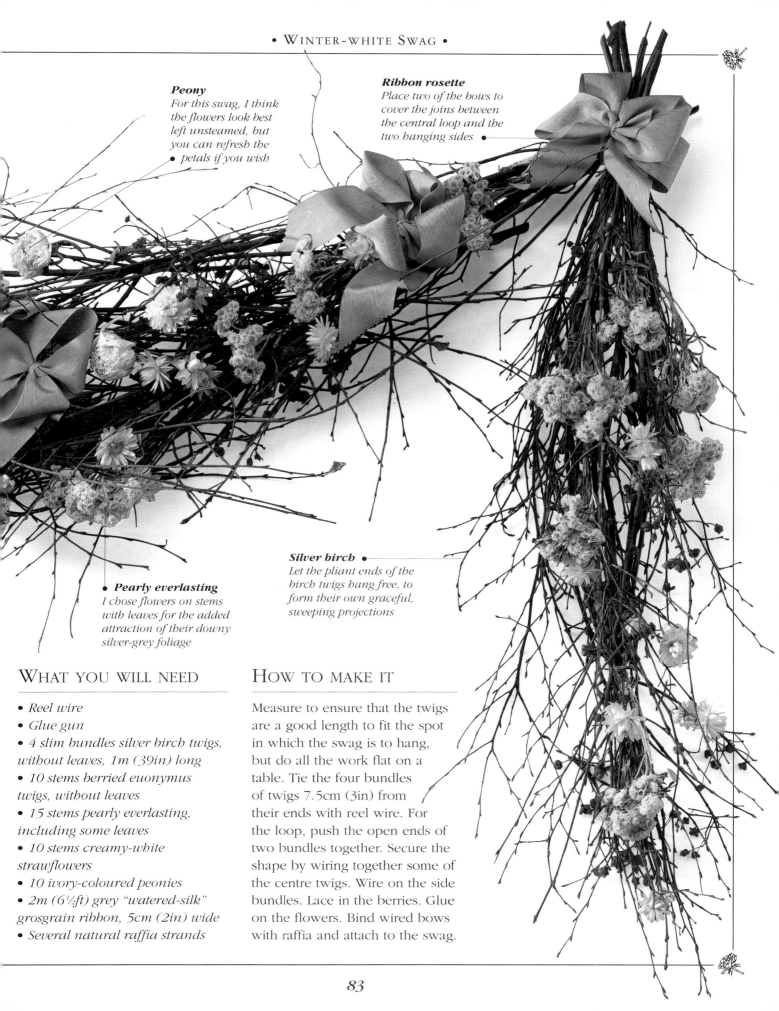

Peony
For this swag, I think
the flowers look best
left unsteamed, but
you can refresh the
● petals if you wish

Ribbon rosette
Place two of the bows to
cover the joins between
the central loop and the
two hanging sides ●

Pearly everlasting
I chose flowers on stems
with leaves for the added
attraction of their downy
silver-grey foliage

Silver birch ●
Let the pliant ends of the
birch twigs hang free, to
form their own graceful,
sweeping projections

WHAT YOU WILL NEED

- *Reel wire*
- *Glue gun*
- *4 slim bundles silver birch twigs, without leaves, 1m (39in) long*
- *10 stems berried euonymus twigs, without leaves*
- *15 stems pearly everlasting, including some leaves*
- *10 stems creamy-white strawflowers*
- *10 ivory-coloured peonies*
- *2m (6½ft) grey "watered-silk" grosgrain ribbon, 5cm (2in) wide*
- *Several natural raffia strands*

HOW TO MAKE IT

Measure to ensure that the twigs
are a good length to fit the spot
in which the swag is to hang,
but do all the work flat on a
table. Tie the four bundles
of twigs 7.5cm (3in) from
their ends with reel wire. For
the loop, push the open ends of
two bundles together. Secure the
shape by wiring together some of
the centre twigs. Wire on the side
bundles. Lace in the berries. Glue
on the flowers. Bind wired bows
with raffia and attach to the swag.

Peony Basket

We're accustomed to putting baskets of flowering plants outside the house, hung on garden walls, but tend to forget that they can become superb decorations for indoor rooms and halls as well. The willow basket that I've chosen for this wall hanging looks rather like a window box, and so I've arranged the dried flowers with their stems upright, to appear almost as if they are growing out of the basket. The arrangement is crammed with texture. Delicate campion and crisp, starry daisies nestle in among voluptuous pink peony blossoms, while the shimmering, leafy oatstalks contribute quivers of pale green freshness that remind me of a wild meadow in early summer.

Cultivated oat •
These pale green stalks are of oats picked and dried before they were ripe; ripened heads are a light honey colour

Peony •
For the very best effect, place these luxuriant flowers at varying heights, from the front through to the back of the arrangement

Pink campion
Nodding catchfly is the quaint alternative name for this plant, which was once a common sight in country hedgerows •

Sunray •
Any daisy-like flowers will do well here, but I chose a Helipterum *species for its coy yellow flower-centres*

What you will need

- *Woven willow basket, 38cm (15in) long, 15cm (6in) wide, & 15cm (6in) deep*
- *8 bricks dry foam*
- *Medium-gauge stub wires*
- *25 oatstalks, including some stalks with leaves attached*
- *12 stems pink peonies*
- *10 stems pink campion*
- *30 stems sunray flowers, in shades of light & darker pink*

How to make it

The basket need not be protected with a plastic trash-bag lining for this arrangement because all the plant material I've used is dried. First, cut and pack bricks of dry foam into the basket so that they are firmly wedged, leaving a gap of 2cm (¾in) between the top of the foam and the upper edge of the basket. Gather the oat leaves and make up several small wired bunches of them *(see page 22)*.

Steam the peonies *(see page 17)* if their petals are squashed. Place clumps of the oatstalks into the basket first, putting some shorter clumps near the front. Add in the wired bunches of leaves. As you are building up the arrangement, remember that its overall height should be about three times the depth of the basket. Position the peonies, and add in the stems of campion and sunray flowers last.

FRUITED HOLLY FESTOON

FRUITS LOOK EXTREMELY JOLLY in garlands and swags, and especially festive when you are making a decoration for the winter holiday season. I've chosen pomegranates for this festoon, together with tamarillos and tangerines, all set among variegated holly. They are such beautiful fruits, in particular those with a deep reddy-pink blush, and their availability has been extended so that you can still buy them right into midwinter. The darkly red skins of the tamarillos are also stunning. Select your tangerines with care so that you get the brightest orange fruits.

WHAT YOU WILL NEED

FOR EVERY 1M (39IN) OF FESTOON
• *1m (39in) chicken wire, 30cm (12in) wide*
• *12 large handfuls damp sphagnum moss*
• *Reel wire & stout stub wires*
• *40 sprigs variegated holly*
• *8 pomegranates, sprayed gold*
• *12 tamarillos*
• *4 firm-skinned tangerines*
• *1m (39in) metallic gold wire-edged ribbon, 4cm (1½in) wide*

HOW TO MAKE IT

This festoon is made on a RIGID BASE *(see page 26)*. Roll the chicken wire around the moss to create the base, making a wider section at the bottom of each loop. Prepare the pomegranates, and wire and stuff them with absorbent paper, as described below in the annotation. Wire the tamarillos *(see page 22)*, and the tangerines as for limes *(see page 88)*. Layer holly sprigs into the base, then wire in the fruits. Attach a ribbon bow at the apex of each loop.

• **Preparing pomegranates**
Cut out a 2.5cm (1in) hole at the base. Use a teaspoon to remove the insides. Push one bent stub wire through the top of the fruit. Stuff the shell with absorbent paper

Holly
A much-loved part of
the winter landscape,
Ilex aquifolium – *the
English holly – gives
us many variegated
• named cultivars*

Tangerine
*Fruits enclosed in tight,
firm skins are the best to
use, because they'll hold
the stub-wire fixings well
and will last longer than
• those with loose skins*

Frosted fruit •
*While it's still wet,
sprinkle the gold
paint with grains
of coarse sugar to
get a frosted effect*

• Ribbon embellishment
*Add tails and spirals of
ruffled ribbon, as well
as multi-looped bows,
for a specially grand
and opulent festoon*

• Tamarillo
*Often called tree tomato,
this fruit not only looks
wonderful, but also has
edible, juicy, succulent
flesh with a tantalizing
sweet-savoury taste*

NUT AND CITRUS TREES

A CHRISTMAS TREE THAT HANGS ON A WALL always excites the most enthusiastic comment. My related pair is quite easy to put together, though as they're somewhat time-consuming, plan to start them a day or two before your festivities begin. The backing of blue spruce branches ensures that the trees will last for a couple of weeks or more, and will hold onto their needles even when the foliage has dried out. You can decorate your own tree in any way that you might dress a standing Christmas tree. I've chosen an interesting and vivacious colour scheme of yellow-green fresh limes mixed with silvered walnuts and passion fruits. Both look very special set against the dusky blue-green of the spruce. Miniature white tree lights enhance the silver sparkle, and give the whole creation a magically festive appearance.

WHAT YOU WILL NEED

FOR THE LARGE HANGING TREE
- *Chicken wire*
- *Mossing wire*
- *Damp sphagnum moss*
- *Medium & stout stub wires*
- *Glue gun*
- *One set miniature white electric tree lights*
- *8 fresh limes*
- *7 passion fruits, sprayed silver*
- *20 walnuts, sprayed silver*
- *3 large branches blue spruce*
- *Piece of bark, for the trunk*

HOW TO MAKE IT

This wall-hanging is made on a MATTRESS BASE *(see pages 30–31)*. Cut sections of chicken wire to form a triangular envelope 60cm (24in) tall, 50cm (20in) across at the base, and open on one long side. Stitch the sections together with mossing wire, then stuff with moss to make a 2.5cm (1in) thick mattress. Stitch up the open side. Push one stout stub wire through each lime, then loop it back in to secure it. Push one medium wire

into each passion fruit. Do the same with the nuts, securing the wires with a dot of glue. Now, starting at the base of the triangle, layer in pieces of blue spruce foliage, with the fronds facing downwards. Overlap the sprays so that all the stems are covered. Make holes in the mattress from the back with a pencil. Push single lights through to the front. Attach the bark, and fruits and nuts *(see pages 30–31)*.

Small hanging tree •
You can make a tree of any size by following my instructions for the large tree: simply remember to keep the proportions the same when you scale them down or up

Fresh lime •
Deep green fruits may look prettier, but these sharp citrussy-yellow ones stand out well against the foliage

Bark tree trunk •
Pieces of bark are sold at good florist's shops and garden centres

Passion fruit •
The skin is a marvellous dark purple, so silver the fruits on their tops only, and sprinkle them with a frost of coarse sugar before the paint dries

Blue spruce crown
When you're layering in the foliage, form a circle of shorter sprays close to the top, then crown the tip with a longer piece that sticks straight up

Silvered walnuts
Spray the nuts all over a couple of times (let dry in between coats) to give them a richly • lustrous finish

White tree light
My silvery scheme looks best set off with white lights, but traditionalists may want to use coloured ones

WINTER HOLIDAY WREATH

RED AND GREEN are the vibrant colours of the winter season. We see them displayed, resplendently, in the rich tones of glossy evergreen leaves and brilliant scarlet berries – colours that look forward to the renewal of growth that comes with spring. Used by the Romans to accompany gifts and as an ornament during the festival of Saturnalia, berried holly is to my mind the quintessence of red and green. In this jolly holiday wreath, I've used it together with clusters of chincherinchee, pieces of blue spruce, velvety anemones, variegated foliage, larch twigs, and scarlet plume, for a contemporary interpretation of the traditional colour scheme.

WHAT YOU WILL NEED

- *35cm (14in) diameter circular wet foam wreath base*
- *Medium-gauge stub wires*
- *20 red anemones*
- *3 branches blue spruce*
- *3 stems* Euonymus fortunei *'Emerald and Gold'*
- *3 branches lichened larch twigs*
- *3 stems leafless berried holly*
- *10 stems creamy-white Arabian chincherinchee*
- *5 stems scarlet plume in flower*
- *2m (6½ft) striped green, red, & gold silk taffeta wire-edged ribbon, 7.5cm (3in) wide*

HOW TO MAKE IT

Soak the wet foam wreath base in water until the foam has taken up enough water to be damp all the way through. Do not oversoak it, or the whole thing will drip when it is hanging up. Bind a stub wire around the top of the base. Bend

Variegated euonymus
'Gold Tip' and 'Sunspot' are attractive alternatives for this green-gold foliage

Lichened larch
These twigs are especially cultivated to promote the growth of lichen: look for them at flower markets or creative florist's shops

Anemone
Replace tired blooms with fresh ones after a day or two – they don't last well out of water

the ends into a loop for hanging up the finished wreath. Wire the anemone flowers *(see page 23).* Arrange sprigs of the blue spruce and euonymus, and short lengths of larch and holly twigs into the ring, in a single direction – here, anticlockwise. Add the anemone flowers in groups, then pieces of Arabian chincherinchee, to make an informal yet balanced pattern. Place sprays of scarlet plume last. Attach a five-looped ribbon bow at the top, with other single and double bows where you please.

Blue spruce
Luxuriant and full,
the foliage provides
a festive and gently
aromatic backdrop
for the flowers

Scarlet plume
This evergreen euphorbia
carries its tiny bracteated
flowers in arching sprays
from winter into spring

Arabian chincherinchee
The flower centres contain
black ovaries – a stunning
contrast to the pale petals

Berried holly
I chose winterberry (Ilex
verticillata), a deciduous
holly that bears clusters of
bright red berries on bare
twigs all through winter

Winter Holiday Wreath

*Find time, in the midst of all
your other preparations for the
festive season, to make at least
one spectacular decoration of
fresh flowers – still something of
a luxury at this time of year.
Sporting gay colours to boost
flagging spirits, its cheery
appearance is guaranteed to
banish any hint of wintry
gloom. The finished wreath will
last for weeks if you hang it in
a sheltered spot outside, or in a
cool room. Just tweak out the
anemone flowers and sprays of
scarlet plume as soon as they
start to look past their best, and
replace them with fresh ones.*

You'll find detailed instructions
for making this fresh flower
wreath on pages 90 and 91.

PLANT DIRECTORY

African marigold *Tagetes erecta* 'Crackerjack'
alstroemeria *Alstroemeria* Ligtu Hybrids
anemone *Anemone coronaria* De Caen Series
anthurium *Anthurium veitchii*
Arabian chincherinchee *Ornithogalum arabicum*
artemisia *Artemisia ludoviciana* var. *albula* 'Silver King', 'Silver Queen'
bell heather *Erica cinerea*
bells of Ireland *Moluccella laevis*
blue spruce *Picea pungens* f. *glauca*
borage *Borago officinalis*
bottlebrush/callistemon *Callistemon beaufortia sparsa, C. citrinus* 'Splendens'
bread wheat *Triticum aestivum*
bun moss *Grimmia pulvinata*
campion *Silene pendula*
carnation *Dianthus* 'Master Stuart'
carpet moss *Mnium hornum*
celastrus *Celastrus orbiculatus*
celosia cockscomb *Celosia argentea* 'Cristata'
chrysanthemum *Chrysanthemum carinatum* 'Monarch Court Jesters'
cluster-flowered everlasting *Helichrysum italicum*
cone wheat *Triticum turgidum*
copper beech *Fagus sylvatica* f. *purpurea*
cornflower *Centaurea cyanus*
cornus *Cornus alba* 'Elegantissima'
craspedia *Craspedia globosa*
creeping Jenny *Lysimachia nummularia* 'Aurea'
cress *Chenopodium aristatum, C. polyspermum*

cultivated oat *Avena sativa*
cypress *Cupressus*
delphinium *Delphinium consolida* 'Blue Bee'
dogwood *Cornus alba* 'Elegantissima'
Dutch rush/mare's tails *Equisetum hyemale*
English oak *Quercus robur*
euonymus *Euonymus fortunei* var. *radicans* 'Emerald and Gold'
euonymus *Euonymus fortunei* var. *radicans* 'Silver Queen'
euonymus/spindle *Euonymus europaeus* 'Red Cascade'
euphorbia *Euphorbia fulgens*
fennel *Foeniculum vulgare*
feverfew *Chrysanthemum parthenium*
field poppy *Papaver rhoeas*
fishtail palm *Caryota mitis*
freesia *Freesia* x *kewensis*
galax *Galax urceolata* syn. *aphylla*
gerbera *Gerbera jamesonii*
globe artichoke *Cynara cardunculus*
globe amaranth *Gomphrena globosa*
gloriosa lily *Gloriosa superba* 'Rothschildiana'
golden rod *Solidago canadensis*
golden wattle *Acacia longifolia*
grape hyacinth *Muscari armeniacum*
Guernsey lily *Nerine bowdenii*
gypsophila *Gypsophila paniculata* 'Bristol Fairy'
hebe *Hebe* x *franciscana* 'Variegata'
holly *Ilex aquifolium* variegated cultivar
honesty *Lunaria rediviva*
hop *Humulus lupulus*
houttuynia *Houttuynia cordata* 'Chamaeleon'
ivy *Hedera helix*
larch *Larix decidua*
larkspur *Delphinium consolida*
laurustinus *Viburnum tinus* 'Eve Price'
lavender *Lavandula spica*
lemon-scented gum *Eucalyptus citriodora*
leucadendron *Leucadendron rubrum*
lichen *Hypogymnia physodes*
lisianthus *Lisianthus russellianus*
love-in-a-mist *Nigella damascena*
mahonia *Mahonia japonica*
Mexican orange blossom *Choisya ternata*
miniature globe thistle *Echinops ritro*

miniature honesty *Lunaria minima*
mop-headed hydrangea *Hydrangea macrophylla*
orchid *Cymbidium, Dendrobium, Vanda*
oriental lily *Lilium* 'Pompeii'
pearly everlasting *Anaphalis yedoensis*
peony *Paeonia lactiflora*
pink pepperberry *Schinus molle*
pot marigold *Calendula officinalis*
prince's feather *Amaranathus hypochondriacus*
privet *Ligustrum vulgare*
protea *Protea* 'Blushing Bride'
protea *Protea compacta*
protea *Protea mellifera*
ranunculus *Ranunculus asiaticus*
reindeer moss *Cladonia rangiferina*
rosemary *Rosmarinus officinalis*
rose *Rosa* 'Europa', 'Golden Time', 'Landia'
ruscus *Ruscus aculeatus*
safflower *Carthamus tinctorius*
salvia *Salvia horminum* Art Shades Series
scabious *Scabiosa caucasica*
scarlet plume *Euphorbia fulgens*
silver birch *Betula pendula*
silver gum eucalyptus *Eucalyptus cordata*
smilax *Asparagus asparagoides*
snow-in-summer *Euphorbia marginata*
Spanish moss *Tillandsia usneoides*
sphagnum moss *Sphagnum auriculatum* var. *auriculatum*
spindle *Euonymus europaeus*
statice *Limonium sinuatum*
strawflower *Helichrysum bracteatum*
strelitzia/bird-of-paradise flower *Strelitzia nicolai*
sunflower *Helianthus annuus*
sunray *Helipterum roseum*
sweet marjoram *Origanum marjoram*
sweet pea *Lathyrus odoratus*
tree asparagus *Asparagus meyeri*
tuberose *Polianthes tuberosa*
tulip *Tulipa* 'Angélique'
viburnum/laurustinus *Viburnum tinus*
weeping willow *Salix* x *sepulcralis* 'Chrysocoma'
wild clematis/old man's beard/traveller's joy *Clematis vitalba*
winterberry (deciduous holly) *Ilex verticillata*
yarrow *Achillea filipendulina* 'Coronation Gold'
yellow kangaroo paw *Anigozanthos flavidus*

INDEX

ACKNOWLEDGMENTS

Author's Acknowledgments

I would like to give great thanks to my partner, Quentin Roake, who has worked with me to produce this book; to Dennis, Dave, and Lee at John Austin, New Covent Garden Market, for all the magnificent flowers that they have supplied; to Machin and Henry at Creekside, South London, for their wide selection of dried plant material; to Stephen Hayward, for all his wonderful photographs, and a plentiful supply of doughnuts; and to Gillian Roberts and Debbie Myatt, who have made working on this book so pleasurable.

Publisher's Acknowledgments

Many thanks to Mark Bracey for computer support; to Deborah Myatt for the line artwork; to Mel Roberts for all his editorial help; and to Alex Corrin for the index.